Pursuing the Untamed

Soulful Discoveries Sipped From Vintage Alaska's Wilderness Goblet.

Douglas C. Myers, Ph.D.

Foreword by Norman D. Vaughan

Since 1978

PO Box 221974 Anchorage, Alaska 99522-1974

ISBN 1-59433-022-0

Library of Congress Catalog Card Number: 2005900636

Copyright 2005 by Douglas C. (Doug) Myers, Ph.D.
—First Edition—

Author may be contacted regarding oil paintings,
additional copies of *Pursuing the Untamed*,
book signings, and public appearances at:
AdventureAlaska_Ltd@yahoo.com.

Manufactured in the United States of America

— Dedication —

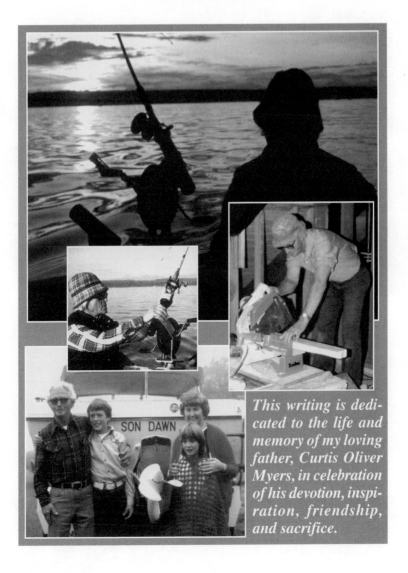

This writing is dedicated to the life and memory of my loving father, Curtis Oliver Myers, in celebration of his devotion, inspiration, friendship, and sacrifice.

— Foreword —

Throughout my life I have known an enthusiasm for risk and a satisfaction from each adventure accomplishment. In *Pursuing the Untamed*, my friend, author Doug Myers, reflects the same spirit. Many of the experiences he writes about reminds me of my own adventures. While reading, I found myself sharing in the details of each event. The passions talked about are the same that promoted my own wilderness pursuits. The theme presented throughout of surrendering to adventurous desires is what I know to be important in daring to dream big.

Pursuing the Untamed describes in interesting detail the instinctive behavior of several of Alaska's wild creatures. Accounts of the salmon's spawning ritual and encounters with brown bears are interestingly informative. For those readers not familiar with such experiences, the book offers a good understanding of instincts specific to Alaska's wildlife.

I am also impressed with Doug's writing about Alaska's Native people. It is a personalized account that emphasizes the harmony between Aleut and Yup'ik cultures, their subsistence efforts (including the use of the ulu knife), and a hospitality that is uniquely Alaskan.

Doug's dedication to discovery is one I know to be essential in living a full life. It was a pleasure for me to read each chapter with a desire for more. I especially enjoyed his thorough account of the annual winter Iditarod trail race and work with sled dogs.

When describing his wilderness adventure experiences, Doug effectively humanizes the wild creatures and events in order to illustrate the essentials in living a fulfilled life. I recommend *Pursuing the Untamed* to anyone who appreciates a sensitive, thoughtful understanding of Alaska's wilderness, its Native people and culture, and wildlife.

Norman D. Vaughan

About Norman D. Vaughan

Colonel Norman D. Vaughan, age 99, was a member of the first Byrd Antarctic Expedition in 1928 - 1930. He was the first American to drive sled dogs in the Antarctic. Mount Vaughan was named to honor Norman by Admiral Byrd for his contributions to the Byrd Antarctic Expedition. In 1994 he returned to the Antarctic where he drew attention to the preservation of the Antarctic and promoted a healthier more active life by climbing his namesake, Mount Vaughan, 10,302' at age 89. The celebrated event was witnessed by National Geographic Explorer.

Vaughan served in World War 11 in the U.S. Army Air Corps, which latter became the Department of Search and Rescue. He participated in the Battle of the Bulge with 209 dogs and 17 drivers (mushers), and commanded the dog sled ambulances used for the rescue of wounded soldiers. Norman also instigated the rescue by dog team of 26 air crews on the Greenland ice sheet, and recovered a top secret Norden bombsight single-handedly. He concluded his term of service with 425 dogs under his command. He later became Chief of Search and Rescue for the North Atlantic Division of the International Civil Aviation Organization (ICAO), the air wing of the United Nations. In the Korean War, he served in the Psychological Warfare Department, assigned to the Pentagon.

Vaughan participated in the Dog Racing Event of the 1932 Olympic Games. He has mushed in 13 Iditarod Sled Dog Races in Alaska, and was awarded the Most Inspirational Musher Award and True Grit Award (1987). In 1990 he was named Musher of the Year. His last finish was in 1990, at the age of 84.

Since 1997 Vaughan has organized an annual Serum Run to commemorate the 1925 dash to Nome following the same Iditarod Trail when anti-toxin serum was delivered using dog sleds to hundreds of dying Eskimos stricken with diphtheria.

Norman's motto in life is: *Dream Big and Dare to Fail*. His writings include, *My Life of Adventure* and *With Byrd at the Bottom of the World*.

http://www.adventurequestinc.com

— Contents —

To Adventure's Best

Doug

2022

Author

(Photo by Toshiko Ihle)

An Alaska resident, Douglas C. (Doug) Myers, Ph.D., was raised in Oregon, where trout fishing on the McKenzie River in the Cascade Range was an indulgence revisited each spring. During academic pursuits in Southern California he remained committed to his fishing avocation. He learned the art of fly-casting on famous Hot Creek in the distant Sierra Nevada Range, and fished extensively clear-flowing trout streams throughout the Eastern High Sierras. His return to the Northwest supported professional objectives and provided fishing opportunities for resident and migrating salmon in waters of Puget Sound. He also fished the famed Skykomish and Stillaguamish Rivers for migrating steelhead trout.

Myers served professionally many years in agency and private practice settings. Prior to living in Alaska his tenure in the state of Washington included Director of Family Court, where he collated and published a research project for the Snohomish County Court of Domestic Relations. As a licensed practitioner he served as a consultant and counseling therapist encouraging reconciliation, personal growth, and relationship sensitivity. Doug is the father of Todd Douglas, avid rock climbing enthusiast, and Colette Dawn, who prefers equestrian trails and warm southern beaches.

In 1984 Myers invested financially in an adventure opportunity of the heart. He became joint owner of a rustic fish camp located on a remote river system in Southwest Alaska. His delight in Alaska's virgin landscape increased with each bush plane excursion. Several of his adventures were shared

11

with Native friends at their historic village site in the region of Bristol Bay. These visits and others in areas of the Bering Sea, the Alaska Peninsula, and Kodiak Island offered cultural insights, fascinating sport-fishing experiences, and close encounters with Alaska's renowned brown bear. Alaska's Southcentral Susitna drainage and Kenai Peninsula regions also provided the author with pleasure to his arm as a sport fisherman and inspiration to his eye as photographer and artist. As an adventurer, the author was privileged to realize the joy that springs from personal fulfillment. As an artist, Myers' goal has been to illustrate on canvas Alaska's scenic treasure, historic Native culture, and wildlife display. Individuals who have tasted Alaska's raw cultural and environmental servings can again savor the pleasure by reading these narrative accounts and/or viewing his oil paintings.

For the vicarious admirer of pristine Alaska, the author's paintings elicit an appreciation for its most valued resource— the spirit of adventure. Each oil painting was painstakingly created in realistic detail. Myers' formal art training was in illustration design at the Art Center University in Los Angeles, California. His progress as an illustrator of Alaska's Native people and wildlife was critically reviewed by acclaimed Alaskan artist Fred Machetanz, now deceased.

A newspaper columnist wrote of an artist who discovered peaceful renewal in Alaska's wilderness. The article titled "The ART of PEACE" was written about the author, Doug Myers. It was a published account about a psychotherapist who for many years helped others recover their passion for living. In writing about people and places that shape life, the columnist explored with Myers the intrigue of the last frontier and how his oil paintings bring to life with paintbrush and palette knife Alaska moments rarely experienced:

For Myers, renewal comes in the wilderness of Alaska with a fly-fishing rod in hand and a camera in his backpack ... In his work, he helped others find healing peace; in his avocation, he has found it for himself. He says his studies of Alaska offer a remote wilderness experience that touches the very core of life. ... hundreds of memories feed his spirit and connect him to the wild and scenic land that is his home.

Linda Bryant, Columnist

— Acknowledgments —

Alaska Natives were influential in the writing of this adventure narrative. Friendships established in Southwest Alaska's bush have been profoundly inspirational. The hospitality of Levelock Natives John and Mary Tallekpalek, Deafy, Charlie Andrews, and Evan Chukwak at their village and historical subsistence site was particularly influential to this writing. I remain humbled by their courtesy in exemplifying the best of Alaska.

I am thankful for the assistance of Alaska Natives Jennie Dorothea (Tunguing) Apokedak and her mother, Jennie Katherine (Link) Tunguing, of the village of Levelock. They were instrumental in distinguishing through translation the Native language dialect of the Aleut-Inuit used by Mary Tallekpalek and other local Native allottees. Jacqueline Villasenor of Anchorage, her aunt Anna Desousa of Bethel, and Kelly Lincoln of Toksook Bay, assisted in the translated use of Yup'ik Eskimo words and phrases native to John Tallekpalek and influential in the formation of the Native language used by the Levelock community.

Nonaboriginal Alaskan friends contributed to the preparation and presentation of my romantic dance with the spectacular. The work of William Schneider, Ph.D., Curator of Oral History, University of Alaska at Fairbanks, served a corroborative role. Sam E. Daniel of Girdwood, supplied technical support. Marthy Johnson of Copyediting Services of Anchorage, strengthened the text presentation. Toshiko Ihle of Anchorage, assisted in excess during the final collating phase. The "Foreword" by Colonel Norman D. Vaughan, world renown explorer and adventurer, is a generous and cherished contribution. Others remain anonymous while having served as a source of positive influence.

I am also deeply grateful for the loving influence of family members. The heartening support of my daughter, Colette Dawn, encouraged confidence. Immeasurable also has been the emotional sustenance offered by dedicated parents, Curtis and Midge Myers. Because of my loving father I will always recognize the radiant, gentle smile and giving hand of a devoted heart. A journeyman by trade, Dad knew love's reward through an enduring spiritual resolve of generosity, patience, and sacrifice. His strength of character is reflected in the countenance of a tolerant and unpretentious Alaska Native, and in shadow lines gracing Alaska's ageless mountain faces. It is also observed in the spawning salmon's rigorous commitment to a purposeful journey. Life's final upstream rendezvous provided my dedicated father a peaceful transition.

Although left behind, and knowing no return to the sea, Mom's pledge to love's requirement has remained firm. I have known strength in sacrifice because of unselfish, persevering parents. Their hearts remain united, even though the shadow movement below the surface current has slowed in revealing but one. To both, I am eternally thankful for their diligence in living a heartfelt life. The nutritional offering left from their successful journey together has guaranteed a life of love that will live forever.

Faithfulness has been my reward with devoted friends Charles E. (Chuck) McDonald, James A. (Jim) Miller, and Lester L. (Les) Carney. Chuck has been a lifelong companion, and both Jim and Les emerged as dedicated friends from post-graduate and professional circles. All three men have contributed an endearing and sustaining influence in my life. Each has shared my most pained and gratifying moments, including adventure experiences described in this composition. Their nurturing friendships have filled potholes of sadness, regret, and failure with comfort, understanding, and inspiration.

— Commemoration —

James A. Miller was a confidant and colleague of international repute. He was acknowledged as a skillful counseling therapist/trainer by professionals in several countries. Jim was highly regarded for his gentle spirit and intuitive understanding. An emotionally caring man of passionate resource, he was dedicated to the pleasure and fulfillment in being fully alive through a heart-connected life. His devotion to love's call and its requirement of surrender was an inspirational source for all that knew him.

Jim shared in my first Alaska adventure on the Alagnak River where we thrilled to the strike of salmon in both shallow and deep current. In life's main stream we were grateful for the buoyancy offered by the other while forging despairing depths together. For Jim, a father's love was tested in a most horrific way. Having given so much in pursuing life's fullness, despair from the accidental death of his only son, Steve, was his torment. The later joy Jim felt with a surviving daughter, Karen, encouraged a rehabilitated heart.

Jim remained very encouraging of this writing for a significant part prior to his death. His legacy to me includes the desire and confidence to embrace life by seizing the moment, and that truth in living is discovered in the heart. An affectionate man like my father, I will forever speak with both men at river's edge, and wherever the soul seeks warm renewal. Their caressing influence has provided a clearer, less rigorous trail to follow.

Jim's sensitive style is further honored here with selected favorites from his preferred inspirational reading of BIRDSONG – RUMI:

Love is that that never sleeps, nor even rests,
Nor stays for long with those that do.
Love is language that cannot be said, or heard.

The way of love is not a subtle argument.
The door there is devastation.
Birds make great sky-circles of their freedom.
How do they learn it?
They fall, and falling, they're given wings.

Lovers in their brief delight gamble both worlds away,
a century's worth of work for one chance to surrender.
Many slow-growth stages build to quick bursts of blossom.
A thousand half-loves must be forsaken to take one whole heart home.

Jelaluddin Rumi, Poet

Prologue
—— Spirit of Adventure ——

Exploring untamed regions of Southwest and Southcentral Alaska was a personal quest for a spirited connection through discovery. Passion's palate savored adventure's vintage wine sipped from a wilderness goblet. Selected memoir accounts reveal affectionate disclosures of remote Alaska's Native people, habitat, and wildlife.

The narrative is written for the outdoor devotee, culturally curious, and searching romantic who embrace the suspense in wild and reverence for the pristine and historic. For some, it provides the vicarious realization of an elusive dream. All will feel the freshness in new discovery. Stitched throughout the written fabric are soulful revelations couched in metaphors and imagery.

Popular books such as *The Last Frontier* and *The Call of the Wild* are testimonials to an intrigue with the untamed. This writing proclaims the invitation of Alaska's wilderness spectacle with a resounding *call to surrender*. Each descriptive experience embraces a giving in to desire's fascination with a more curious, courageous, and fulfilling life experience.

Clothed in natural beauty, the undisturbed habitat is a timeless treasure discovered by a fortunate few. Grand landscape spectacles that attracted eighteenth century global circumnavigator Captain James Cook persist today, including those of the inlet named after him. Wilderness pleasures are woven into a tapestry of discovery and compromise. Seductive sights and sensuous scents of pristine freshness speak of an alluring land with a preserved past. Remote settings beckon an inquisitive heart. These experiential disclosures serve as an alternative to the familiar and mundane in a developed world. For the author, inspiration has led to dedication. The reward has been nature's warm caress as she beckons to her bosom with the youthful innocence and modesty of a virgin.

The written drama unfolds with an inauspicious introduction to bush Alaska. A dream-come-true opportunity was challenged by the realities of deception and disappointment, and later by emerging sentiment. It was the best and worst of the Alaska dream! Subsequent accounts include: Goodnews discovery and renewal in a promised land; seeking subsistence by Native Alaskan friends at their historical fishing site; wild river moments of solitude, comradeship, revelation, and reward between father and son; a volcanic peninsula's wildlife symphony of sights, sounds, and slashing silver leading to a discovery of abandoned village artifacts; seagoing sourdoughs willing to risk everything in prospecting a glittering promise; a lost-world island setting where close encounters with brown bear demonstrate instinctive extremes of savagery and nurturing; less remote access to compelling scenery and wildlife displays exhibiting love's requirement; dogged determination during a dashing Iditarod experience, and a musher handler's account; and the tandem occurrence of winter's frozen splendor and summer's bounty of fragrant renewal. Finally, understanding passion's call *as* a last frontier enables pleasure's freedom song (Epilogue).

The writing portrays with narrative privilege rare and exciting experiences that illustrate Alaska's cherished resource—the spirit of adventure. Heartfelt discoveries were written with the dedication of a passionate pen. Anecdotal material will inspire a seeking heart, and call to action the fulfillment of ambitious desires and dreams. While honoring the pristine wildlife habitat it describes, the book will hopefully encourage a greater appreciation for its enhanced protection. Personal observations and resulting insights are aided by training in psychology, religion, and the arts.

Similar to the narrative accounts, cherished impressions accenting wild discoveries in remote Alaska have been memorialized on canvas using oils, brush, and palette knife. The genius of each painting is its reflective expression of passion's adventurous pursuit. Several photos of the author's oil paintings, including the two appearing on the book cover, are available for viewing in the "Appendix". Interspersed throughout the text are photographs taken by the author, unless otherwise indicated.

ADVENTURE   ALASKA

Katmai's Other Eruption

Best and Worst of the Alaska Dream

During the year 1912 violence visited Southwest Alaska. Mount Katmai's snowcapped peak once dominated an impressive Aleutian Range skyline. On June 6, a colossal eruption collapsed its majestic reign of the upper Alaska Peninsula. Immense geologic turmoil resulted in a cataclysmic face-lift. The natural catastrophe changed forever the environmental character of the Bristol Bay drainage system.

Since its calamitous ruin Mount Katmai's immense volcanic crater and surrounding area have remained free of any major geologic disturbance. Katmai's Valley of Ten Thousand Smokes remains a passive monument. Through renewal the region has re-established ecological interdependency. Recovery has been realized in the re-creation of a pristine wilderness mecca that is world renowned. Wildlife, indigenous Alaskans, and adventure enthusiasts have since benefited from the genius in nature's restoration.

The nearby Alagnak River system has been both a survivor and provider of the untamed wilderness drama. The river originates from clear Nonvianuk and Kukaklek Lakes, located within Katmai National Preserve boundaries. Its link to the Kvichak River and Bristol Bay provides one of the largest annual runs of migrating red (sockeye) salmon in the world. It also offers ideal spawning grounds for large runs of king (chinook), silver (coho), pink (humpy), and chum (dog) salmon. The Alagnak River was included on a short list of Wild and Scenic Rivers in Alaska. In addition, the upper section of the river is a designated trophy region and part of Alaska's wild trout management program. It is reputed to be one of the best native rainbow trout fisheries in Alaska. Because of the pristine character of the upper river it also offers excellent grayling fishing.

During the winter of 1984 I invested in a remote fish camp situated on a high bank overlooking the Alagnak River. The investment goal required a joint venture agreement with the existing owner and manager of fishing operations. My primary function as new joint owner was to manage the financial interests of the business while assisting in its operation. We agreed to develop a struggling fish camp into a prestigious lodge facility for the dedicated sport fisherman. The original name had been selected because of its proximity to the famous Katmai National Monument and Preserve.

My investment seemed attractive, reasonable, and promising based on annual salmon migration counts and a projected favorable Native land lease agreement. It did not appear to be the response of an avid sport fisherman's heart alone. Essential to our future success would be a satisfactory work environment at the fish camp site and the successful extension of a land lease agreement. The existing owner affirmed that conditions influencing both concerns were encouraging. By contingency agreement all declared circumstances affecting the operations of the distant fish camp were subject to my personal on site review and verification at the beginning of the following sport-fishing season.

Prior to my arrival at the remote river location, however, a nongeologic epicenter of conflict within the area was traced to a high bank along the Alagnak River. Ominous dark clouds of discontent cast a forbidding shadow on the Bristol Bay drainage below. Emotional tremors were felt the length of the Alagnak and Kvichak Rivers.

The United States Government had granted aboriginal property rights to allottees of Levelock Native origin along both river shorelines. However, the Bureau of Land Management did not provide for the sale of property allotments to *outsiders*.

A lease-only provision for the commercial use of land was considered a temporary safeguard against predacious investor dealings with a naïve Native community. During the prescribed period of protection Native allottees and/or Native corporations could profit only through the agreed use of their land. Such a lease agreement was the precursor to conflict between the Levelock Native Corporation and my managing partner. It became a human relations catastrophe.

The conditions of discontent were never revealed leading up to the signing of my joint venture agreement or during my preparations to visit the remote site. Contrary to owner representation, pressure had been building downriver with the Native council. Several payments on the land lease agreement remained unpaid. The Natives' reward for patience was broken promises resulting from bad faith personal guarantees. Native dissatisfaction grew with each successive default payment. The prolonged pattern of promise followed by nonpayment was as well received as an intruder in the path of a bull moose during rut. White man's deception and arrogance fanned the flames of contempt within the Native village of Levelock.

The word Katmai was again prominent in expressing a profound concern for the stability of the area. It eventually became a rallying cry. Corporate Native elders relied on ancestral instinct in dealing with such cunning. A chorus of humming motors sounded a stealth advance across the great width of the Kvichak River and entrance to the tributary Alagnak River. Boats filled with angry, determined young Natives armed with rifles gave witness to a clandestine occasion. Authorized by the Native council, young men with warriors' intent navigated several miles of a winding remote waterway. The objective was to take possession of land leased to the fish camp owner as a cure for the pain of deception.

As the small armada advanced farther upriver it was heard at the fish camp site by the owner and site manager. With the strategic skill of a cavalry officer my new partner ordered the employees to form a line in front of the fish camp at the highest level of the bank parallel to the river. Each employee was positioned with a guide's shotgun readied to defend against the Native advancement. Tranquillity of a remote setting was challenged by an organized armed staff and howling sounds of approaching boats. Guns were raised with a single purpose on both sides. However, with the determined grit of my partner's show of retaliatory force the Native mission failed. On that occasion the preparedness of the encamped whites served to discourage any continued effort by the committed Native combatants.

Returning to the council of elders, the frustrated messengers learned of a second mission. In an effort to avoid injury or loss of life they advanced their appeal to a courtroom in Anchorage many air miles away. A municipal court hearing was scheduled for a later date during the fishing season on behalf of the plaintiff allottee and Levelock Native Corporation.

Unaware of my new partner's deception and the recent Native effort at property recovery, I embarked on a commercial airline to Southwest Alaska's outback, which seemed the fulfillment of a dream. I was greeted at the small King Salmon terminal by a robust bush pilot. Van Hartley, owner of Branch River Air Service, provided bush commuter flights for our fish camp. He was my first Alaska exposure to the new business operation.

At the frontier outpost of King Salmon perishable produce and building materials were transferred to a single-engine Cessna floatplane waiting at the nearby Naknek River shoreline. Passenger luggage, supplies, and materials approached the cargo weight limit for a small floatplane

The deafening sound of a strenuous river lift-off was quickly forgotten while we circled the Naknek River at very low altitude. We could see below legions of migrating salmon darken the river's clear water. My excitement rose to a level higher than the plane was capable of flying.

Our flight course was charted to cross an expansive tundra between the commercial outpost we left and the remote fish camp site on the Alagnak River shoreline. The noisy, slow-moving plane provided my first viewing in the wild of breeding pairs of white trumpeter swans and several individual migrating caribou. The silent members of nature's wilderness community introduced a serene episode of intrigue. The view from our plane served as a connection to what appeared to be a timeless creation. It seemed that the developed, civilized world had fallen off the horizon's edge behind us.

From the plane the Alagnak River's braided course was viewed running through a lush tundra flat-land fed by the mineral rich Katmai National Preserve region. A Native trapper's cabin was observed near the river's edge.

When approaching the fish camp site below the pilot circled with a friendly dipping of the plane's wing to announce our arrival. Through the small window and blurred rotation of the single-engine propeller I could see people gathering on a high bank in recognition of our coming. Staff workers waved in a welcoming motion as we glided toward the river's silvery surface.

A revved single engine moved our floatplane across the river to a gathered few. While taxiing the wilderness water runway I felt the excitement of having won a lottery.

After the floatplane was secured to the riverbank I carefully stepped from the cabin onto one of the pontoons. Cautiously walking a narrow wood plank spanning the clear, slow-moving current I noticed large native rainbow trout strategically positioned in the water below to pounce on discarded salmon remains drifting from the fish camp cleaning bench upstream. In the ecstasy of this angler's realized dream, Alaska's remote wilderness drama and display was no longer a fantasy.

Imported totem poles from Southeast Alaska had an exotic appeal in front of a roughly built lodge

Naïve enthusiasm characterized my greeting to the staff, as it had previously with the floatplane pilot in King Salmon. Each employee was welcoming, but expressed an ambivalence toward my role as a new owner. Although hopeful, none felt confident that my addition would improve existing circumstances. The fishing guides, camp cook, and floatplane pilot all complained of a volatile work setting due in part to nonpayment of salaries. Resentful of the owner's breach of promise, most were prepared to abandon their working contract for a return flight to the Lower 48. As a result, vital business operations were at risk. My immediate response was to pay each according to their agreement for services.

Federal regulations for the protection and enhancement of the Alagnak River's status as Wild and Scenic were being violated as a procedural matter. Polluting practices, together with management's personal improprieties and supervisory conduct, created an unfavorable working environment observed by the staff and later by guests. So much for pleasant working conditions!

Joint ownership left no doubt with the Native council regarding my reputation as partner. I soon learned of the Levelock Native Corporation's emotional disposition regarding our lease agreement and our noncompliance-defendant status in court. Furious, the president of the Levelock Native Corporation rejected my request for a conciliatory meeting. Feeling disenfranchised, the Native council communicated clearly its intention to have no further dealings with my disingenuous manipulating partner or his associate.

A favorable court decision for the plaintiff would have certainly resulted in the immediate closure of our fish camp operation. Because of my partner's cunning testimony, including additional promises and the appearance of contrition, the judge substantiated the existing lease contract as viable. The attempt by the plaintiff Native group to secure a court-ordered remedy for the broken lease agreement had failed.

Although I remained dismayed by the circumstances requiring our litigious defense, my initial investment was rescued from certain loss. However, there appeared to be no merit in further attempts to negotiate an extension beyond the current lease agreement. My partner's court promise of capitulation had little influence with an already victimized village people. Acts of guile and intrigue over integrity violated a trustful environment, and became a cancerous influence. The Native community's contempt for such reprehensible behavior infected all stabilizing efforts at reconciliation. Without a continuing lease agreement there was no chance for future survival. So much for a favorable Native lease extension!

It therefore seemed certain that neither a satisfactory work environment at the fish camp site nor an extension of the lease agreement with the Native corporation would be possible. The growing prospect of divorcing myself from a wilderness setting that nourished a longing for more was heartbreaking.

Remote Alaska's appeal was not diminished by regret, however. Countless hours spent designing, constructing, and implementing improvements to the river-based fishing lodge remained fond memories. The distinctive aroma of smoked salmon being prepared for the arrival of fishermen in camp was a testimonial to the earlier construction of a smokehouse without the aid of a level or plumb line.

Above the kitchen-dining entrance was inscribed Drift On Inn. A hand-carved paddle donated by a German party floating the length of the river was placed above the sign in memory of shared pleasantries during their restful visit.

Other indelible experiences were cradled between the steamy scent of early morning coffee and an Alaska sauna's nighttime flickering flame. Everything that transpired was a testimony to the discovery of richness in remote. Large lodge windows revealed an accompanying setting sun that reached across a reflective river to reverent hearts.

Soulful music played by talented river guides provided the ambiance of a sacred folk performance. Their unison bowing and plucking of violin and guitar paid honor to the late night's colorful calm and to those transfixed by its mystique.

At a fly-tying bench skillful hands manipulated feathers, Flashabou, and thread during the casual concert. A melting of personal ambitions between guests of varying backgrounds encouraged mutuality and comradeship. Morning's fishing reconnaissance downriver gave evidence of the previous night's successful fly-tying efforts with ecstatic shouts of "Fish on!" Gratuitous handshakes cemented friendships following thrilling moments shared by anglers on the river.

Notable individuals, including retired Boston Red Sox slugger Carl Yastrzemski (on the left) enjoyed a peaceful escape from the residual requirements of popularity. Holding a king salmon with a congressman friend, he was later inducted into Major League Baseball Hall of Fame, 1989.

During an especially memorable week my dear friend and colleague, Jim Miller, participated in the realization of a dream. Our lives had melted together through years of mutual interests, parenting, and personal growth. As fathers we raised together an older son and younger daughter of the same ages. We had been to each other an inspiration in seeking life's fulfilling pleasures and a source of support and comfort during life's greatest disappointments.

When Jim arrived by floatplane I felt the joy in knowing a loving, devoted brother. His affectionate support and generous spirit remained a treasured gift of life. At airports he was occasionally mistaken for the main movie character portrayed in the television adventure series *Grizzly Adams*. During the week that followed I scheduled a private showing of much of the river's length. Similar to other occasions in the Lower 48 robust enthusiasm vacillated between awe and laughter. Time together on the Alagnak River provided additional memories of love's deepest calling between friends.

During our exploration downriver we left the boat to wade through shallow water directly across from a Native subsistence fish camp site. While fly-casting for chum salmon we were enchanted by the cultural ambiance. Included in the historic visual ensemble was a corrugated metal shed used for curing salmon with smoke escaping to the sky. Other abandoned outbuildings rising above the height of bear grass signaled a previous time of village activity. The occasional barking of sled dogs punctuated an enduring past. I later became good friends with Native elders John and Mary Tallekpalek, who with Native elder Deafy continued the site's subsistence food gathering for the Levelock Native people.

Jim Miller's arrival at the fish camp was a warm reunion.

The view across slow-moving, reflective waters was of a birch pole fish-drying rack weighted with hanging salmon.

The pounding of chum salmon against our legs redirected our attention downward to a migrating multitude around us. With cheerful laughter and joyful exuberance we continued fly-casting maneuvers, giving less attention to skill. The salmon were aggressive and apparently not distracted by our position in the water. Jim's pleasure was unabashedly expressive with each explosive take of his personally designed purple and pink ugly streamer fly tied the previous night.

After successfully catching and releasing many salmon we left the shallow water with tired arms for other challenges upstream. Earlier Jim landed several large king salmon during his week's stay. On this day we boated to calm, shallow backwaters away from the main river current where torpedo-shaped northern pike rested. The aquatic predator's instinctive profile includes ambushing unsuspecting smolt (small salmon) migrating downriver to an open sea. With the physical characteristics of a barracuda, the pike is no less ferocious. Each stealthy pursuit by the slender assailant resulted in an explosive surface attack of our moving patterns. Shouts of ecstasy punctuated thrilling battles as we reveled together.

My gratitude for Jim's devoted friendship seemed heightened by the circumstance of a remote environment accessed only by small boat or bush plane. During his departure I felt a profound loss as the floatplane taxied its watery runway, leaving behind the extended gentle caress of my dear friend. With greater distance the diminishing roar of the revved single engine preparing for lift-off solidified the feeling of solitude. At river's edge I remained softened by an affectionate spirit, and the influence of Jim's continued presence. The pain in longing was a reminder of love's requirement.

While pensive, I experienced a tearful view of the floatplane rising to a height downriver where it disappeared from sight.

Indelible memories are evidence of a pivotal life experience challenged by the darkness of disappointment. A plethora of beckoning sounds, sensuous sights, and enriching exchanges were overriding features that accompanied the second Katmai disturbance. Similar to its geologic predecessor of 1912, from the bowels of turmoil came peaceful renewal. Inspiration's creative influence transcended painful illusions and loss. Soulful revelations refreshed the spirit as a lover's embrace does the heart.

My initial dance with the heavens survived a decision to exercise the contingency provision in the joint venture agreement. Regardless of my partner's bad faith behavior, my committed interest in Alaska's untamed wilderness remained undiminished. While befriended by Native friends with sharing hearts downriver, I wrote a new song that left no doubt of my return.

Message of Goodnews

—— Promised Land ——

My disheartening debacle on Alagnak's riverbank eventually translated into good news. The following winter off-season provided encouraging correspondence with Levelock Native friends seeking an alternative to the existing turmoil on the Alagnak River. In order to learn more of fish camp/lodge operations in bush Alaska I contracted with river tent camp owner/operator Ron Hyde of Alaska River Safaris (later changed to Goodnews River Lodge). My position was assistant manager of operations at the remote fish camp's western Alaska location.

Access to the distant river-based fish camp required a bush flight from the outpost village of Bethel south along the Bering Sea coast. With earplugs in place, the vista was a silent view through a window of a commuter mail plane. The surface below appeared like that of a moonscape. The tundra was dotted with countless glistening lakes and ponds extending to Kuskokwim Bay and the Bering Sea beyond. Eventually, an enormous body of water pointed inland to snow-covered peaks of the Ahklun Mountains, extending from Cape Newenham National Wildlife Refuge far into the Togiak National Wildlife Refuge. On the distant coastline a Yup'ik Eskimo village next to a braided river that fed the enormous bay was sighted. Yup'ik, or Yupiit, means *real people*. These discoveries were indeed good news, for Goodnews was the name given the village, river, and bay. History's paintbrush created a distant village of indigenous people with simple, lasting strokes. Sparsely spaced dwellings were weathered by generations of harsh environmental conditions, especially abrasive winds off the Bering Sea. Shacks spewed thinly scattered trails of white smoke drifting softly upward toward an extended blue sky.

Stationed on a tundra shoreline, the small rustic village of Goodnews Bay faces the bay with the same name and its Bering Sea connection.

Because the Goodnews River also defines the village boundary, a bountiful subsistence resource is extended upriver from the bay.

The village landscape was interspersed with strewn, discarded items that had served a critical need for survival. Rusty barrels and old wood boats dominated the land scene. Crowded conditions also included piled and hung fish nets, buoys, outboard motors, four-wheelers, power generators, and scattered parts for each. Leaning against the crude wood structures were winter sleds for mushing, walrus skulls with ivory tusks, and whale bones.

Lines of fishnets drooping between horizontal poles along the beach and drying fish hanging from open-sided wood shacks were displays of a resourceful and successful fishing village.

Draped over small supply sheds were inverted bear hides. Covering much of the corrugated metal roof, the drying skins were edged with brown and blonde fur from underneath.

Large sections of butchered bear carcasses hung from thick ropes at the rear of roughly built huts. Numerous air-cured seal pelts were stretched against the flat surface of rustic exterior walls. Other spoils from successful hunts were exhibited throughout the village.

Located near some dwellings were head markers of wood that gave evidence of Russian Orthodox influence. A villager of position was memorialized further with a small white picket fence bordering the grave location.

Because much of the subsistence fishing and hunting was done at sea, an inordinate amount of space was required for the dedicated village cemetery. In addition, a sandy beach served as a suitable resting place for wood-planked fishing boats that had survived a treacherous sea. Other craft that knew nothing of survival resurfaced only at low tide.

Barking Eskimo sled dogs tied separately to a stake next to an animal hut symbolized an enduring village experience. The dedicated husky breed echoed a culture's primitive link while unifying it with the present. Intermittently, the timeless ambiance was transformed to modern by revving four-wheelers en route to the village store/post office or by motorboats waiting at shoreline. The roaring engine of a mail/commuter plane also challenged the usually tranquil setting of piled and draped fishnets, drying fish, animal skins, and large area of grave markers. The noisy contributions of an outside industrial world's engineering success distinguished the disparity between ancient and modern. Considering technology's influence in the enhancement of both cultures, however, it seemed an acceptable distraction.

From a peaceful village setting at high tide I traveled by jet boat up a narrow, winding, Goodnews River into the heart of the Togiak National Wildlife Refuge. My destination was a distant tent-camp location inaccessible by floatplane. A primitive river landscape emulated the Garden tranquillity of time's beginning. The safari excursion was more awe-inspiring than any entertainment adventure park replica.

A gentle, inviting river awaited a multitude of migrating faithful fresh from the Bering Sea. The salmon's surge upriver was programmed to preserve its past by securing its future. Every predator linked to the quiet river was awaiting a deluge of spawners. Evidence of recent bear kills in the village downriver suggested a small margin of error for salmon swimming near the shoreline in shallow water. A tenacious brown bear alone could deny several struggling survivors a successful mission. Caution in navigating or wading near the river's edge was equally important to the humbled human species. Fresh brown bear paw prints in muddy sand along the shoreline was a daunting revelation, even for the meek. Pleasure's gain in pursuing the untamed did not include risking aggressive jaws of plundering, ravenous furry giants along riverbanks.

Crafty, less menacing opportunists below the river surface were patient for returning salmon bearing gifts. Among the waiting, native rainbow trout sensed the certainty of a succulent offering. Without the forbearance of resident trout, Dolly Varden char felt instinct's urge for a reconnaissance downriver of swarming salmon entering from Goodnews Bay. For the subsurface scavengers a percentage of discharged roe (eggs) was the price for salmon-spawning rights.

The secluded tent-camp was in a remote setting showcasing the wild in wilderness. Smooth water in front of the fish camp splashed with schooling Dolly Varden awaiting a later charge downstream.

At the distant river camp, world fly-casting champion, Steve Rajeff, instructs guests on the art of fly-casting.

The fish camp's electrical needs were supplied by ground-mounted solar panels angled to the sky. Radiant energy was collected from the atmosphere and transmitted to charging batteries. Flat, black surfaces seemed less intrusive to nature's pristine landscape than the harsh sound of a gas generator motor. No noisy device was stationed within the camp to distract from the seduction in serene or disrupt the healing in tranquil.

*Tents for sleeping were erected on wood platform founda-
tions. Guest quarters were in line with a larger commissary
tent for community eating and supplies.*

*The camp cook was fitted in white during dinner. His chef's
uniform included a tall mushroom hat that suggested a gour-
met serving. Each prepared meal, followed by fresh-baked
desserts, was commensurable with such excellence. It was
well established that for guests fishing the river it was also
good news at the dining table.*

41

The arrival of sport fishermen at the remote fish camp accompanied a parade of preoccupied salmon surging upstream. A majority of guests anticipated testing arm strength against a few of the determined heavyweights. For others, a wild and robust rainbow trout of unusual size was the challenge of choice. Popularly referred to as 'bows, the celebrated monarchs flourished as caviar-seeking opportunists. Protected by regulations, the freshwater icon delighted in nature's wild river pantry of spawned salmon egg preserves. Catch and release of the square-tailed ruler of the upper river region guaranteed its continued reign.

For the wild trout aficionado, long, willowy fly rods arched against hunger's explosive take. Airborne 'bows flashed sides streaked with crimson in an aggressive, acrobatic display. Vivid battles and respectful releases fulfilled ambitious dreams of the gracefully dedicated fly-fishing angler. For the fly-casting devotee, memories of challenging freshwater aerial displays in the upper river shortened long, tiring flights home.

My wilderness trek to the distant Goodnews River embraced a message of promise and renewal. While standing next to the distant river leading to an expansive Bering Sea, soulful music played the previous year from a high bank along the Alagnak River had not diminished, nor had the dream faded. The Goodnews River was an opportunity to gain experience in operational logistics for such a venture. Previously befriended by Levelock Native allottees, I was encouraged to consider the development of a guest sport-fishing operation along the lower Alagnak River. As a result, reliance on hope was lessened by an increased aliveness through discovery.

ADVENTURE ALASKA

Seeking Subsistence

—— Ancient Privilege ——

Native villages throughout Alaska have relied on subsistence gathering as a food source for countless generations. Ancient privilege among Native groups within the Bristol Bay region of Southwest Alaska has preserved an extended past in harvesting the environment's sustenance resource from generous to marginal. Neither seasonal uncertainties nor calamitous events have altered age-honored practices in the collection of berries and preparation of fish and wild game. Staple provisions from subsistence gathering include salmon, trout, caribou, moose, bear, seal, walrus, and whale.

Not until 1971 was culturally claimed Native property granted ownership status in support of subsistence by the United States Government. Regional corporations, including the Levelock Native Corporation, were established to settle aboriginal land claims. The Alaska Native Claims Settlement Act provided perpetuity of ownership through government allotment.

The Katmai village of Levelock is located on the west bank of the Kvichak River ten miles inland from Kvichak Bay and forty miles north of Naknek. It is located near the Kvichak River's tributary Alagnak River Wild and Scenic Corridor. Early Russian explorers used the word Kvichak when referring to the village of Levelock. It's mixed heritage is comprised of Aleut-Alutiig from the south and Yup'ik Eskimo from the north and west.

Inherent property rights for the Levelock Native Corporation and its people included the length of the tributary Alagnak River. Historically, some indigenous villagers from the Levelock Native community on the Kvichak River lived separately along the banks of the Alagnak River. On the lower river a subsistence fish camp site once bustled with family life that included several village shacks and a church. A provision of the 1971 Native Claims Settlement Act stipulated that allottee children must have a formal education. Consequently, the relocation, or return, of families to the main village site on the larger Kvichak River was necessary to comply with the educational requirement for children. Because the rivers are connected, a link persists between the aboriginal Levelock village location on the Kvichak River and historical Native rights embedded in the meandering shorelines of the smaller Alagnak River.

The Native designation of the Alagnak River is Branch River. The popular local name suggests the river's many branches, or braids. Outsiders familiar with the Alagnak River refer to it as the Branch River, or the Branch, in conversation and writing. Branch River Fish Camp is the name given the historic shoreline section of the Levelocks' subsistence village site left behind.

The abandoned village and remaining subsistence fish camp commemorates a timeless, age-honored culture.

During my several visits all the structures remained as they had been prior to the relocation of the villagers to the larger Kvichak River site. A monument to Russia's missionary influence stood on a nearby raised slope overlooking a tundra and river landscape, accentuated by the subsistence gathering fish camp at river's edge. The far north edifice remained a retired sanctuary next to a white-picket-fenced graveyard. White markers designed with the Orthodox symbolic cross gave evidence of the buried village faithful. Three iron bells varying in size were hung on the outside of the church. The heavy bells had previously served commercial fishing vessels on nearby Kvichak Bay. Ropes from the bells were extended through a side window to serve a bell ringer inside the one-room church building. Each pull of a rope, or ropes, sounded a distant invitation to solace worship up and down the river.

Above the entrance a weather-beaten sign read, Branch River Russian Orthodox Church.

47

Inside the sacred house priestly articles of sacrament and celebration appeared ready for continued service. A worn Yup'ik translation of the New Testament Gospels, including Psalms, was centrally placed on a rustic wood altar for community worship.

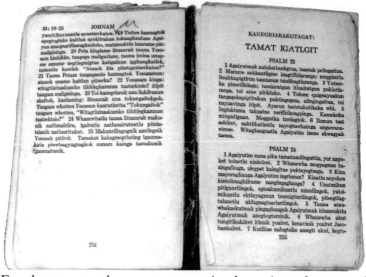

For the converted, repentant, or simply curious the opened Bible served as a source of inspiration and comfort.

Near the church rusted corrugated metal shacks were what remained of a once viable village site overlooking the Branch River Fish Camp and river landscape in both directions. A community sauna built low to the ground was mostly hidden in tall bear grass. Because of the bathing hut's height it was necessary to bow to enter. Such respectful posturing seemed an appropriate requirement considering the sauna's sacred status and spiritually cleansing climate available inside. While inside the confined cubicle it was easy to imagine generations of Natives monitoring meditative moments to purge the soul. Sweaty dialogues describing bear encounters, prosperous caribou hunts, success in reaping fur pelts along the river, or a generous offering of returning salmon must have been stimulating to the weary. The sauna was a sanctum where wood-planked walls, water-stained rocks, and a metal drum stove absorbed generations of steamy exchanges. *Maqiluk* is the Native-Yup'ik word to invite someone for an Alaska sauna, or steam bath. *Maqinaurtukut* is used when the invitation includes more than two people. Following relocation of the small extended village site, obscurity replaced vital village customs. Left behind were bald eagles, moose, and brown bears to forage throughout the deserted gathering place.

Distinguished Natives from the Levelock community on the shore of the Kvichak River maintained the pulse of the satellite village's historic cultural past. Seasonal subsistence fishing at the Branch River Fish Camp was done by ancient influence. As guardians of the ways of the Levelock, they contributed the most to subsistence gathering for the main village on the connecting Kvichak River. Sport fishermen and adventure seekers familiar with the Branch River Fish Camp affectionately referred to the site as John and Mary's fish camp.

Preserving the old ways of their people based on careful observation and subsistence were husband and wife John and Mary Tallekpalek.

The distribution of labor was simple for the elder couple. John managed setnets along the river's edges, collected fish caught in the nets, hung fish for drying and smoking, and with extended family member Charlie Andrews repaired by hand damaged nets. Regular maintenance of the nets was required because of the persistence of aggressive salmon, very large beaver, and scavenging brown bear. Mary often participated in the checking and picking of fishnets. A signature sight on the river was of John and Mary tugging at nets from the edge of their small open boat along the river's shoreline.

The Tallekpalek's marriage was of Yup'ik Eskimo and Aleut Native cultures. John was originally from the north where he was born at the Eskimo village of Pilot Station on the lower Yukon River. Mary was born at nearby Big Mountain, Iliamna.

John performed tasks associated with catching and preserving the salmon.

Chores exclusive to the elder wife seemed exhaustive. Mary did the splitting and filleting of salmon from each netted catch. She was highly skilled with her ulu knife, a curved metal blade. John fashioned the handle by hand from the bone of a beaver. It was the only form of knife Mary ever used. After Mary completed the split filleting of fish, John would hang them on an air drying rack made of birch wood poles. The cross-pole design included several horizontal poles for hanging fish and suggested the frame structure of an elongated teepee. Dipping the fish in staple seal oil was another ancient procedure used by Mary in preserving salmon for winter use.

Following the preparation process, fish remains were gently dropped into a steaming metal drum of boiling water heated by a wood fire. The ancient recipe for protein-rich mush provided a principal food for sled dogs. When in season whole chum salmon carcasses were used. Native use of the lesser regarded chum salmon to feed their dogs is considered the origin of the

Time spent by Mary next to the river in a bent-over position using a cutting board table appeared arduous.

slang *dog salmon.* Also, of the five species of salmon the chum has canine-appearing teeth most similar to those of a dog.

(Photo by Ken Caraway)

During visits to the fish camp the offensive odor of brewing fish parts often required a greater distance from its source.

51

In addition to being air dried, salmon were often cured over molten coals inside a corrugated metal smokehouse next to the drying rack.

On one occasion a ponderous brown bear foraging for food interpreted the unpleasant steamy aroma as an inviting alternative to its river shoreline surveillance. The bear advanced toward camp like a relentless tax collector in search of overdue payment. Preserved meat was stored in a raised cache and safe from the bear's plan to plunder. However, other tantalizing morsels that hung from the fish drying rack added to the dinner bell appeal of the boiling bonanza. Unison howling by camp sled dogs alerted us to the approaching menace, even at some distance. When the chorus alarm changed to intense barking we knew the scavenging hulk had crossed camp boundaries.

Husky sled dogs were individually tied to a post with a short rope. Only John and Mary's two favorite dogs were able to run the fish camp site unfettered. Both with black fur, one was a large Lab and the other a tiny mixed breed. The shaggy little mutt was Mary's special pet. The appearance of a huge brown predator encouraged John's Lab to join in protest with other nervously barking huskies, but only after establishing a safe distance.

Stimulated by the smell of salmon bisque, secretions of saliva cascaded from the undulating lips of the bear's lower jaw. During this tense and unpredictable time I understood the naming of Mary's pet, *Bear Dog*. Seeing the enormous bear the wee mongrel assumed the tenacity of a ferocious guard dog intent on deterring a pirating thief. Incessant yapping irritated and confused the intruder. Like an annoying *no-see-um* mosquito, the mutt's persistent nipping at the bear's heels provoked the lumbering creature to seek relief in trees at the edge of camp. In retreat the humbled giant appeared bewildered as to its pillaging role and the size of a tiny defender's heart.

The small mixed breed was central to another incident resulting from Mary's instruction. During one of Mary's sojourns by riverboat to the main village of Levelock the matted mutt silently inched through the open doorway of the Tallekpalek's rustic shack to scrounge for food. I was unable to redirect the slithering beggar outside as requested by Mary. The dog's confused eyes were its only response to my command in English. *Outside* (of the hut) was not a word it understood. However, after being instructed by John on the use of the Yup'ik word *ellami* (*enem elatinun-pi* in Native Levelock) the dog's disciplined return to the front porch was immediate. In other villages it may be pronounced *keggani* or *gagani*. *Ellamun anluni* is also used, meaning *to go outside*.

Bear Dog was not allowed inside the Tallekpalek's rustic shack.

Later, I experienced as occasions of privilege evening conversations with Native family members. Evan Chukwak from Levelock and Mike Andrews with his wife from Igiugig near Lake Iliamna traveled by boat to visit with elders John and Mary Tallekpalek, Deafy, and Charlie Andrews at the Branch River Fish Camp site. All were family or extended family on Mary's side, and as allottees maintained river property rights within or near the subsistence fish camp location, the place of their origin. I vacillated between mesmerized and stimulated while listening to hunting, fishing, and survival stories of Native Alaskan proportions. The reunion was a demonstration of Native family solidarity. Dialogue with each member also provided me with additional instruction regarding their synthesized language.

From left to right: Mike Andrews wife, Mike Andrews, Evan Chukwak, Charlie Andrews, John Tallekpalek, and Deafy.

The use of Native Levelock words and phrases were helpful in speaking with Mary, who spoke more comfortably in her Native tongue. I learned to use *Camai* (pronounced *Jami,* and spelled *Cama-i* in Yup'ik) to say *Hello* or *Hi*. If I added *ca-pia*, then my greeting was curious as to what was going on. To ask Mary how she was feeling (*How are you?*),

I used Native Levelock words *qaill-ayugsit?*. The Yup'ik equivalent is *Cangacit?*. To be able to say *Erneg assirtug unuamek* (*Ellakegciu* or *Ella assirtug unuamek* in Yup'ik) for *It's a nice day today* complemented our connection. The Native word *kuuvviaq* was more recognizable, and therefore easier to say when requesting coffee. Distinguishing between salmon processed for subsistence by Mary at the fish camp required the use of *taryaqvak* for king salmon, *sayak* for red salmon, and *qakiyaq* for silver salmon. Also harvested for lesser use were chum salmon, *aluyak* (*iqalluk* in Yup'ik), and pink salmon, *amaqaiyak* (*amaqaayak* in Yup'ik). When arriving at the fish camp for subsequent visits, *Akanek tangeqsaitamken* (*Tangeqsailkemken tang akanek* in Yup'ik), meaning *I have not seen you for awhile*, and *Yuarnakamken*, meaning *I have missed you*, were difficult statements for me to pronounce. *Guyana*, meaning *Thank you*, and *Kenkamken,* meaning *I love you*, were much easier to speak when leaving.

It is important to note that the composition of Native language words and phrases vary between villages depending on traditional use and neighboring linguistic influence. The dialect of the Alutiig sub-group of Aleut from the south of Levelock is different but compatible with the Yup'ik language of the north and Western Alaska. For the Aleut-Inuit community of Levelock the local Native dialect emerged from a confluence of these separate languages.

Deafy was another elder Native dedicated to the ancient ways of the fish camp during seasonal subsistence efforts. Appearing voiceless and with no formal education his life was confined to the watershed environment of bush Alaska. Deafy was affectionately named because of a congenital auditory condition. He was born without the ability to hear with his ears, and knew mostly silence his entire life. However, from his responsiveness while standing at river's edge, he was apparently able to sense approaching boats by feeling vibrations through water and from the ground. Beyond his exuberance as a proud overseer of the river's resource and dedicated contributor to subsistence gathering, his actions transcended physical limitations and demonstrated a confidence in social skills.

Deafy's cabin of corrugated metal was adorned with caribou antlers. The rustic metal-clad shelter was his place of birth, and where he stayed each summer while working the subsistence fish camp.

At approximately five feet Deafy's small stature seemed impressive.

Deafy was an inspirational acquaintance and served as a skillful river guide during each of my visits to John and Mary's fish camp. His cryptic vocabulary was etched in sounds of grunts and sighs. On one occasion while I was awaiting the arrival of a floatplane for my return flight to the bush outpost of King Salmon, my elder friend grunted a message of his quick return. He had noticed my movements in concert with recorded music being played through a headset from a Walkman player.

Following his return I was amazed to observe him carefully remove from a plastic bag two harmonicas different in size. It was easy to imagine that these instruments held a special place near Deafy's heart. To imitate music he pressed his mouth against the silver metal of the larger one. With the aid of uncertain hands he blew soulful sounds of no melodic familiarity. However, the tone-deaf musical message transcended his human condition and the preference for a melodious performance.

Our relationship had been so endearing that the prospect of my leaving on the plane in the sky, as he would motion with his hand, motivated him to seek a final connection through music. While forcing his breath through the flat mouthpiece I saw in Deafy's affectionate eyes a moist message of regret. His inner voice transcended the harsh musical display. The spirited effort was not of performance, but a boundless display of courage, tenacity, and loving purpose. My heart was quickened to revere the elder Native's sensitivity and warm embrace.

The occasion was a gift of love, a profound spiritual encounter where cultural and genetic differences had no voice. I was

(Photo by Ken Caraway)

Standing together, as a Native of fortune Deafy spoke with a smile, excitement in his eyes, and mysterious motions.

humbled to experience profound tenderness from a disadvantaged Native man who knew no limits. During those measured moments, the world beyond remote fish racks of drying and smoking salmon, howling sled dogs, and boiling fish carcasses did not exist.

Deafy's speechless condition belied his loving capacity free of distortion. The resonating sounds of silence shadowed his every move. For this solitary soul there was no need of compassion. A silent world protected him from verbal criticism and condescension, soothing sounds indeed. His weather-beaten face was wrinkled by seasoned smiles and joyful tears of heartfelt times. Deafy's voice in history remains absorbed in the fertile banks of the Branch River for all seasons, and echoes a privileged sound to all who knew his spirited pride.

In observing Deafy's adaptive style I could not help but reflect on the silent, loving expression that was my father's. Integrity, patience, and service distinguished both men. As with my father, cherished experiences were highlighted by the simple, generous, and genuine. Deafy, together with extended family members at John and Mary's fish camp, personified the best of bush Alaska's hospitality. The memory of all is etched forever in time.

ADVENTURE ALASKA

River Wildlife Potpourri

Adventures of Father and Son

Sharing the adventure of bush Alaska can be a time of personal bonding reminiscent of frontier solidarity. To experience this enchanting land for the first time with my son, Todd, was a memorable occasion for both. Our journey together began with a flight from Anchorage to an outpost airport facility in Alaska's Bristol Bay region. Magnificent clear panoramas of the jagged and glacially endowed Alaska Range, Northern Aleutian Mountains of Katmai National Monument, and expansive Lake Iliamna provided an enticing precursory display during the flight.

At the outpost village of King Salmon supplies and gear were loaded into a floatplane at the edge of the Naknek River. We used Branch River Air Service for our air taxi needs. Experienced bush pilot Van Hartley served the fish camp I had previously owned on the same river that was our destination.

A smooth lift-off raised expectations of father and son as the plane's instruments directed us to a familiar shoreline fish camp on the Alagnak (Branch) River. Our approach landing on the river's glassy surface was like stroking silk.

While water-taxiing to a waiting John and Mary Tallekpalek we could see through the cabin window and slowing propeller a salmon head mounted on the end of a horizontal pole near a fish drying rack. Native custom required that the head of the first caught salmon be offered in anticipation of a successful fishing season.

Stepping from one of the plane's pontoons onto the ancient riverbank I introduced my son to generous Native elder friends of previous visits. They understood the significance of a young man's curious response to the call of the far north. Elder John shared in soft tones his primitive hand-fishing technique using an alder branch, line, and bare fishhook. This was Todd's first exposure to a remote setting without congestion, computers, or video games. Later, their cordiality focused on preparations for our departure upriver.

Mary demonstrated for Todd her use of the ulu knife for splitting salmon. She also used it for every other cutting purpose.

Leaving the subsistence village site, elder John guided us upriver against currents of excitement and expectation. Our remote rendezvous with bush Alaska continued with a solitary view of slow-moving surface reflections. Bordering willow, birch, and conifer spruce were duplicated in a reflected display along a smooth watery shoreline.

Included in the river reflections was a striking image. It directed our attention upward to an overhanging tree where a mature bald eagle sat high

on regal watch of our intrusive approach. Soon, however, the sighting of an osprey suggested a host less contemplative of our presence. (Eagle photo by Terry Manthey)

Roughly built beaver lodges of great size were located next to the riverbanks. Large beavers worked tenaciously along the edge of the river remodeling lodges damaged during early spring by hungry bears.

The pristine river habitat included moose feeding near the calm, grassy edge. A large mother was positioned to graze between her calf and our slow-moving boat. Because moose usually give birth to two calves, the missing calf probably was the nutritional requirement of a local brown bear. Occasionally, small calves are also lost while attempting to forge swift-moving water. The gentle lower Branch River, however, provided easy crossing.

Following the main river we moved steadily upriver until it narrowed with the addition of several branches. Each of these side channels beckoned the adventurer to enter its serene stillness as a prelude to some wild revelation. Serendipitous discoveries were alluring to both father and son. However, our greater interest was elder John's trapper cabin farther upriver.

Later we approached weathered buildings high on a bank above the shoreline. With the intrigue shared by frontiersmen entering a village site for the first time we stepped out of the boat onto a path used by elder John when trapping along the remote Branch River. I climbed with my son up a steep incline and walked through thick bear grass to our wilderness suite. Outbuildings were stationed in the tall grass and covered with partially rusted corrugated metal. A narrow outhouse boasted a soft toilet seat brought from afar. The tallest building was used for butchering and hanging of moose, caribou, and bear. Inside were stored traps used in collecting smaller fur animals. A sales receipt dated 1948 was discovered listing various furs sold to Mike Aguya:

JOHN N. TALLEKPALEK
Passenger and Freight
Dealer in Furs
Levelock (Bristol Bay) Alaska.

16 Lynx Skins	@	$150 each
13 Wolf Skins	@	$100 each
20 Fox Skins	@	$40 each
30 Beaver Skins	@	$25 each
22 Otter Skins	@	$18 each
98 Muskrat Skins	@ (indistinguishable)	

Another outbuilding was Todd's favorite find. It included an inviting Alaska sauna with rocks and a metal drum for heating.

Father and son preparing for a steamy occasion, a comforting reprieve from insect repellent and residual grime.

The dilapidated, humble trapper cabin was of rustic wood construction with a corrugated metal roof. Weathered and tilted by age, the cabin was also slanted and uneven from harsh environmental conditions and limited foundation support. Built according to Native standards for passage, short doorways required a lowering of the head in passing. A musty interior seemed roughly welcoming. This was especially true when we considered the swarming mosquitoes outside.

From the high bank location our excited eyes became transfixed on awesome territorial scenery. The view through a six-paned kitchen window was stunning. An ageless meandering river with lesser branches lined by trees of deciduous and evergreen was a magnificent terrestrial display of Southwest Alaska's pristine character. The winding river's mild movement encouraged an expanded lush appeal with sloughs lined with bear grass and meadows of spongy moss. Bordering the fertile river drainage on both sides was a vast tundra landscape with sparsely spaced spruce of a spindling type. From the top of a taller evergreen at water's edge a bald eagle contemplated its river reward. Freedom's adopted symbol was later distracted by a territorial squabble with an equally focused osprey.

The kitchen table was covered with level-wind casting reels, pencil lead, and Spin-N-Glo lures with barbless Siwash single hooks for a healthy release while drift fishing. Fly-fishing reels with floating line lay next to an assortment of patterns for resident fish upriver. Purposefully packed fishing vests were draped from rustic chairs next to fishing rods, insulated waders, and other equipment. In addition to angling for wild rainbow trout and arctic grayling, we were prepared to explore shallow midriver side sloughs for northern pike. Large colorful streamers of orange, pink, and purple had proven successful in fishing for chum salmon over shallow bars downriver. Deeper-flowing water was more fitting for kings, requiring weighted luring techniques.

While selecting fishing tackle for our trek upriver we heard the hum of a floatplane passing the cabin. At nearly eye level we saw the friendly dipping of the plane's wing. The pilot was the same who had air-taxied us from King Salmon, and knew of our final destination. Our exuberance in exploring some of Alaska's untamed region was obviously shared by others.

The following morning we began our expedition upriver with the use of elder John's boat. The day's dawning revealed a masterpiece composite of wilderness habitat. Kissed by a warm sun, we shared limitless excitement. Startling viewing pleasures accompanied our sojourn to the unexpected. Following a wide bend in the river a pair of gangling sandhill crane bid us good morning as they made a stealthy lift-off along the riverbank. A brown bear reacted to the roar of our boat's motor by hurriedly retreating from the river's edge near moose swimming to reach the shore. It seemed orchestrated by fate as the cow was leading a small-racked bull in a forged river crossing toward the bear's position. Slowing to a trolling speed, we were cautious not to unnerve the moose while edging their swimming effort in the river. We imagined that by boating the river that morning we served a role in the drama of wild creatures.

Only when the moose rose from the water at shoreline were we aware of their enormous size.

Continuing upstream we felt pulled as if by some spiritual magnet. Similar to endless decades of wild river explorations by fathers and sons before us, it was an opportunity for instruction on both subsistence and pleasure. Pristine water conditions in the braids upriver provided a home for grayling and wild rainbow trout. Hungry crimson-to scarlet-streaked trout savagely struck at all egg patterns during a gorging frenzy. Because it was not a matter of subsistence, and in accordance with protective regulations for a wild trout resource, we exercised the art of releasing each catch. I will always cherish Todd's satisfying grin matched next to a proud display of his first-caught colorfully streaked 'bow prior to release.

Remote and beckoning, the solitude experience offered an imagined alignment with countless Native generations past. Agnes Estrada, Levelock allottee, used this cabin for trapping upriver on the Branch River braids.

At the upper spawning ground location rotting carcasses were seemingly endless along the sandy edges of streams. Imprinted in the muddy sand next to fish cadavers were bear tracks, some larger than the size of my cap. It was a reminder of the need for prudence while fishing the remote upper river braids. Stepping from the boat to shore also required caution because of slippery, moldy skins of dead fish layered on the shallow stream bottom. On that occasion a primeval landscape reeking a musty stench was staged for father and son.

The experience we shared dramatized more than a primitive beginning. There was no inconsistency in what appeared a wasted resource. An unlimited depository of decaying salmon belied its nurturing contribution to countless salmon fry (offspring) feeding on the predecessor's remains. While contemplating nature's upper river cemetery we recognized its equally important function as a nutritional nursery. To live beyond survival Alaska salmon must surrender to death's requirement. In awe we reverently observed the principle of necessity, and that abundant life is a gift of sacrifice. Our insightful gain from visiting nature's regenerative display made clear the Natives' understanding of honor with regard to death.

In truth, all suspense is laid to rest with no contradiction or regret. The genius of nature's infinite success is its reliance on opposites and extremes. Whatever is true, its opposite is equally true! A fly-fisherman's forward-cast requires a back-cast (roll-cast excluded). Extended daylight hours during an Alaska summer must abide with a lengthy, darkened night-time winter. Depending on one's location, a vigorous sunrise is for another a tranquil sunset. The coexisting of opposites helps to understand the interdependency of life and death, and the need to surrender to both.

An appointment with traveling kings was scheduled for the following day. Past a fledgling eagle awaiting mother's return we boated to a wider section downriver. In popular water near the river's mouth a final pilgrimage had begun. Guided by smell, legions of chrome-bright veterans of the sea left Kvichak Bay in full regalia to accomplish a fateful return. Royal blue skies heralded a distinguished advance up the Kvichak River to a predestined Alagnak River route. Dressed in hues of silver, copper, and rose the distinctive Alagnak king salmon was imposing in appearance.

Guided fishermen from lodges throughout the Bristol Bay region had congregated by floatplane to entice the magnificent monarchs. Armed with rods and reels we anticipated our joust with the most sovereign of salmon. Light line strength and barbless hooks were chosen to provide greater sport and easier, healthier releases. During the clear day a parade of stately giants moved sporadically but quickly to avoid the sun's penetration in relatively shallow water. Although prodigious in size, king salmon have little eye protection. Sensitivity to light or glaring conditions account for its preference for deeper water. The required ransom of a lingering king was a worthy fight for supremacy. For most, a noble warrior's reward was its release.

Following a marathon battle with one of the transient rulers of the river we decided to keep it for the dining delight of family and friends back home. Similar to previously caught and released fish, it began with the head-bobbing motion by an irritated king capable of launching a powerful, tackle-busting run. My heart throbbed from an adrenaline rush as I pulled back hard against an arched rod. Realizing it was a formidable adversary I proudly shouted, "Fish on!" The tightly stretched line was not designed to stop strong runs by a king of that size. Because we were using lightweight line the impressive fish needed to be finessed with rod tip, loosened drag, and a maneuverable motorboat. Steady, prolonged resistance against the king's forceful effort to escape required patience, arm strength, and skill in handling the boat. The powerful salmon surged from cutbank to midchannel to shallower mudflat conditions farther downriver.

It was the giant king's instinct to return to the river's estuary mouth where it had entered earlier the same day. Caution's challenge was to avoid being pulled farther by the salmon's effort to be free. The large fish was not able to sound, as is its tendency when caught in deeper ocean waters. Limited to shallow tidewater conditions it jumped wildly above the surface in an instinctual display more suggestive of the much smaller silver salmon. Lighter line tension was taut and at risk of breaking with the acrobatic moves of an angry, formidable male. The celebrated hookup was also problematic without an oversized landing net in the boat.

Finally, good fortune appeared on the far bank of the river. A fisherman held his lunch in one hand and the solution in the other. Understanding our plight, the fisherman waved a king-size landing net from his boat. With the coordination of relay sprinters passing a baton we made the transfer while maintaining a firm connection to our noble quarry. The finish line was undetermined, although certainly several hundred yards farther downriver.

Although exhausted from the lengthy battle, the king's final spirited charge ended with a splendid showing near the boat. Its grand features included a sizable girth with the unique  copper hue of Alagnak River kings. Using the borrowed landing net we carefully lifted a magnificent heavyweight buck into the boat. Our legs, arms, and speech quivered with the intensity of an adrenaline overdose. We later returned the landing net upriver to our newly acquired fisherman friend and wilderness teammate. His helpful effort was acknowledged by grateful hearts.

While returning to our trapper cabin suite upriver we were serenaded by a resonating, even-throttled outboard motor. Day's end offered an exhibition of wilderness river images that soothed the soul. Gliding over a golden-pink sky mirrored on the water's smooth surface gave the impression of being airborne during sunset. Only trailing wake lines distorted Heaven's choreographed display of rich colors. Blessed by the peaceful-calm of angler nirvana we felt escorted by more than the riverboat beneath us.

It had been a time for meeting royalty, a gold medal moment cherished by father and son.

Extended contemplation was shared by father and son as inspirational. My wilderness adventures with Todd were invigorating times of discovery and exchange. Throughout, bush Alaska's sweet caress was best exemplified in the cordiality of Native friends, John and Mary Tallekpalek. Each day offered a new canvas and palette of paints for the blending of wilderness images by adventurous spirits.

Forging past John and Mary's fish camp we marveled at its reflected extension on the river's glassy surface. Visual impressions were of historic Native huts for living and for smoking fish, an elevated cache, a sauna outbuilding, and a crosspole drying rack weighted with split salmon. Smoke from the processing shack rose with ancient approval. It was a hallowed place kissed by the setting sun.

While reflecting on our solitude setting and the joy it offered us in being together I recalled a previous excursion beginning at the same river location. It was a flyout to Brooks River Falls, within the Katmai National Park boundaries. I was flown to Lake Naknek near the Land of Ten Thousand Smokes by floatplane pilot Van Hartley. It was exciting to observe an ancient gathering place of marauding predators enormous in size. The national monument and preserve showcases one of the largest assemblies of brown bears in Alaska. Brooks Falls is a mecca for both salmon-gorging bears and wildlife photographers documenting the predator ritual.

Upon our arrival Brooks River was saturated with spawning red salmon. Congestion was not limited to the flowing freeway of frenzied fish. Riverbanks on both sides yielded a large congregation of heavyweight bears sparring to establish, and sometimes defend, a place at the rocky banquet table near falling water. A hierarchy was established that rewarded the most aggressive and persevering. Greedy persistence by assertive veterans of previous campaigns preempted ambitions of the less experienced.

The sockeye were programmed by genetic instruction to secure an honorable fate beyond the falls. In search of destiny's success the unsuspecting red pilgrims were vulnerable to the formidable falls and the reception committee of menacing brown bears guarding it. Hesitation near the base of the falls and attempts at traversing its height made the protein-rich messengers of hope easy prey. For some, an ill-fated jump ended in the snatching jaws of a waiting bear while airborne. Others were wrangled near the bottom with pillaging paws during pouncing attacks.

Each brawny carnivore jockeyed for position in front of or at the top of the falls.

Our return to Lake Naknek required the use of a trail paralleling the predator-crowded river. While nervously walking the path I glanced from the corner of my eye to see an imposing image in the clearing next to the path. It was a huge brown bear, only a few yards away. My visceral reaction imagined its size to be taller than the distance between us. In trepidation I glanced a hurried second look. The bear's fixed, small beady eyes seemed incongruent with the breadth of his scarred head. Knowing that the skull of a giant brown bear can deflect a hunter's bullet, I later imagined the extensive battle resulting from such wounds. The bear's repose did not alleviate my palpitation, and its resemblance to a cuddly teddy bear offered no comfort. I replayed from my memory instructions regarding a close encounter with a brown bear. *Show no fear while talking in a conversational tone* was the pregame strategy. Such gallantry was not easy when legs felt only numbness and the heartbeat was one of survival.

Safely past the clearing, with renewed courage, I reached for my camera to seize the moment. The bear, which I imagined standing, rose from a sitting position before exiting into the trees. Apparently, content with the thrashing of salmon and the red in sockeye, it showed no interest in pursuing a lean paleface.

ADVENTURE ALASKA

Streams of Dreams

—— Alaska Peninsula's Silver-Lining ——

The Alaska Peninsula is infamous for rough weather and harsh living conditions. It is a narrow strip of land with chronic seismic activity known as Chain of Fire. Reminiscent of primeval times, the Aleutian Range extends along a lengthy terrestrial arm that cradles the Bering Sea. Huge volcanic monuments form its geologic spine. From near the base of these decapitated earthen giants emerge pristine streams that flow to estuaries emptying into renowned Bristol Bay of the Bering Sea on one side or the Gulf of Alaska on the other. Large lakes held by spacious crater rims also feed major water routes to the ocean. Each summer and autumn these shallow rivers and streams are reclaimed by hordes of migrating salmon scurrying past commercial and subsistence fishnets near estuary mouths. Upstream from these inlets an occasional angler or resident brown bear witnesses nature's prolific surge. On the Alaska Peninsula, unlike the Kenai Peninsula of South-central Alaska, there are no connecting roadways leading to corridors of combat fishing zones.

During early September, I arrived with my fishing buddy Terry Manthey in Port Heiden via Reeve Aleutian Airways. Terry had previously managed fish camps on the Kenai Peninsula and Kodiak Island. In a single-room airport terminal we met his brother, Ken Manthey, a licensed setnet operator on two river systems that flow from the narrow Peninsula's volcanic mountain range to Bristol Bay. We agreed to assist his brother and managing partner, Ray Wadsworth of Kodiak Marine Construction, with commercial fishing operations on the lower Ungashik and Ilnik Rivers in exchange for bush flight connections, lodging, and sport-fishing access to the rivers. At the peninsula outpost we boarded a single-engine Cessna bush plane with Wadsworth at the controls. Notice-able were the plane's oversized tires, designed for takeoffs and landings on the tundra's sandy river shorelines.

Against a harsh, unyielding wind the course was set for viewing a solitary landscape extended from ages past. The low-elevation flight provided sightings of basking seals and sea lions stationed the width of the Port Heiden Sanctuary at the mouth of the Meshik River below. Wandering cari-bou were also easily spotted against a shimmering mudflat while crossing the estuary at low tide. The expansive un-tamed scenery and sampling of wildlife viewing was a pre-lude performance staged along a Bristol Bay shoreline of black volcanic sand. As we flew near the mouth of our remote river destination there was no mistaking our first camp location from the air. A small, corrugated metal cabin glistened from the sun in contrast to tundra uninhabited by humans. Used mainly for bear hunting, it was the only permanent structure on a marshy landscape of lustrous ponds extending as far as the eye could see. The distant horizon displayed the huge snow-covered volcanic cavity of Mount Veniaminof, elevated above others to oversee both the earthly and heavenly.

Stiffened by an abrasive wind we unloaded fishing tackle and supplies from the small plane at shoreline. A welcoming chorus of migrating waterfowl together with the cackle of flushed resident ptarmigan created a vibrant symphony of ce-lestial and terrestrial sounds. Nature's feathered audition seemed an impressive introduction to a setting reminiscent of time's beginning. As an accompaniment, the constant shrill sound from windswept bear grass and yapping of nearby fox added a primitive charm to a growing wildlife ensemble.

The stimulating spectacle was a purposeful congestion ordered by instinct. The sky darkened intermittently with increasing numbers of winged vocalists joining the concert spectacular while searching for a migratory rest stop. Among the lofty performers were emperor Canada geese in large numbers, graceful white tundra swans, eloquent white trumpeter swans, and spindle-legged sandhill cranes. Crowded conditions along shorelines amplified freedom's song as scores of devoted feathered families congregated in preparation for a long journey south. The gathering of flocks was the wildlife equivalent of a "powwow happening" shared by Native Americans. The grand display was of resounding eloquence, and impressive to the spirited romantic.

Nature's celebration was extended beyond the sensational surround sounds of daytime flight and foraging. Crashing waves onto a secluded, obscure coastline resonated nature's pulse, while a crystal-clear night sky radiated the divine. Heaven's brilliant nighttime performance served as an antidote to temptations of arrogant positioning and pompous pursuits.

Later while we were sleeping, our spiritual unification with the universe was interrupted by rustling sounds outside the cabin. Several sly fox and a cumbersome brown bear seen earlier chose night's darkness to scavenge for food. The nocturnal noises were easily heard through the cabin's thin walls, even with the harshness of a relentless wind. Nervousness from uncertainty encouraged images of a more menacing carnivore intruder than timid canines with pointed muzzles. Deep depressions in a nearby beach the following day confirmed the nighttime

(Photo by Terry Manthey)

The carrion had been some satisfaction to the foraging brown bear near our cabin the previous night.

presence of a ravaging predator. Pawprints led to a headless walrus and a mauled sea otter that had been washed ashore.

A peaceful morning, however, transformed the anxious night into a blissful dawn. Stunning horizontal rays from an emerging sun streaked the calm, marshy tundra. Tranquil sights and sensuous sounds were measured by the Genesis account of time's beginning. A golden sunrise display was complemented by soothing sounds of silence. Harsh winds had hushed, relegating previous tempestuous conditions to a fleeting memory. From near our cabin three trumpeter swans dressed in purity softly elevated skyward above a reflective pond. Rising vapor from the warming pond's surface added to the symbolism of the event. The white swans' gentle ascension upward was by smooth, winged acceleration through the sun's colorful flaring rays. From a less lofty position cackling male ptarmigan hidden below in a thin, misty layer proclaimed the angelic creatures triumphant lift. In addition, an applauding crescendo of sounds from a multitude of resting winged nomads celebrated the rapturous event.

The distinguished raucous sound of sandhill cranes could be heard from a great distance, whether flying alone or flocked together. When concentrated in the marshy mudflat shoreline at low tide their caw was amplified to create a mesmerizing effect. Several stilt-legged sandhill cranes with colorful headdress and plumage remained grounded near the cabin. Ravenous feeding had extended the search from nearby marshes to elevated grassy terrain. The stork-like lift of a dangling-legged sandhill crane lacked the celestial symbolism of a white tundra or trumpeter swan.

The immense gathering of winged migrants was a prelude to the feature performance upstream. Although inspired by overture sounds surpassing chilling tabernacle productions, our main interest in visiting the pristine wildlife monument was to fly-fish for another of Alaska's migratory icons, the robust silver salmon. The trek upstream included a variety of wild revelations that heightened visions of splashing silver. Numerous brown bear tracks along the shoreline, cackling ptarmigan, scurrying fox, and cautiously posturing white tundra and trumpeter swans above a silver lining fresh from the sea were serendipitous discoveries.

Our excitement and eagerness knew no restraint. The wide-angle view was of an untamed place, serene and undiminished by human encroachment as far as each horizon. Camaraderie was a celebration of youthful dreams revisited. We were confident that the swish of our fly rods against the vast Alaska sky would confirm the fulfillment of boyhood ambitions. Although our objective was prospecting slashing veins of silver, it was clear our richest discovery was joyful hearts!

Only a flyover by an Alaska Fish and Game plane during a monitoring of setnets downstream briefly altered the solitary landscape.

The river's surface reflected changing hues of blue and gray from above while shielding a rich deposit of silver below. Each strike produced an adrenaline rush that riveted our attention to the fishing line's cutting action across the stream's surface. The shrill whine of taut line stretched to vigorous salmon was a welcome sound to more than our ears alone. Cautiously, resident red fox began to approach our position on the river in response to the flashing and splashing of salmon. Beyond curious, these cunning creatures anticipated a reward. It was as if some hospitality payment was due them for our use of the river.

Advancing close to our fly-casting position was a crafty, less timid fox seemingly sure of success. However, with each release of salmon into the river's cold water, it became less patient.

The wily critter could only imagine the prize so long as our excitement included both catch and release. (Photo by Terry Manthey)

For the angler there was no delay in recognizing the extent of nature's generous bounty. The soft rustling of scavenging fox nearby in concert with a migrating winged ensemble overhead enhanced a matinee spectacle of splashing silver stripping line from shrill-sounding reels through the eyes of arched rods. From swishing fly line to splashing surface fury, the stimulating drama was a heavenly preview of eternal bliss.

Catching and releasing the famed silver hooknose was our success, sharing a soulful exchange our reward. (Photo by Terry Manthey)

Sightings of other migratory faithful added to the rugged charm of this distant setting. During a brief respite from fishing a shaggy cow caribou and young spindle-legged calf paused nearby at the edge of the stream. Instinctual mapping required the vigilant caribou's safe crossing of the stream near my fishing location. Hordes of silver salmon lay resting in the caribou's watery path to the other side. Startled by my presence the skittish mother did not hesitate to bolt across the shallow stream. A calm, reflective surface was transformed into churning white. Scurrying salmon panicked in response to the predator-like charge above. The wavering-legged calf's effort to follow its mother's hurried crossing and exit up the far bank was awkwardly humorous. Several attempts by the wobbly calf to climb the bank were necessary before it was reunited with its nervous mother waiting at the top.

Later, a majestically racked bull caribou stopped at the same stream crossing location. He possessed all the characteristics of a stately suitor. The salmon that retreated downstream in response to the previous overhead invasion had reassembled. The dedicated silvers were not deterred from completing a purposeful mission upstream. Regal in stature, the bull caribou's response to my presence was more restrained than the frightened cow's earlier, although its preference for solitude was obvious. The salmon again responded to a dark figure above with the instinctual flight reaction required of prey. Dorsal fins sliced wakeful watery paths, crisscrossing the water surface in streaking directions. After the wandering male caribou turned and merged into the vast tundra landscape, the multitude of faithful salmon advanced seemingly undaunted. The silver salmon's perseverance was also exhibited following each successfully placed angler's fly. Exhausted from battling a flyfisherman's desire and dedication, each migrating mating rights advocate continued upstream once released. Distracted only, the faithful focused again on a mission possible.

On a second river system we discovered structural remains of a once viable Native culture. Near our drift-fishing location was an abandoned Aleut village obscure in its claim to history. The village was evacuated by North Pacific operations during World War II. Japanese forces had occupied nearby Aleutian Islands of Attu and Kiska. Consequently, the villagers of Ilnik were removed from their Alaska Peninsula ancestral surroundings with no preparation for leaving or provision for returning. Resentment flared because of the arbitrary decision to evacuate and incorrigible conditions during the distant protective encampment. It's compliance with United States military strategy resulted in longing hearts that searched for proud footprints in the sand. The government-sponsored disenfranchisement resulted in bitterness for some that lingered with age.

The ghost-like Aleut village remains a monument to a controversial past. An empty one-room Russian Orthodox Church containing religious artifacts stood as a reminder of a more memorable time. Liturgical paraphernalia seemed to be in suspended preparation for the return of the converted village faithful. The rustic sanctum was stationed on a remote tundra landscape of windswept tall grass and prolific pink fireweed. During decades of persistent harsh winds the weathered sanctuary of spiritual refuge had remained steadfast. Red fox constituents not included in the hurried evacuation continued to perform the watchful duties of the departed.

A spirited but ravaged Native past was also embodied in the village's severely weathered wood-planked buildings with corrugated metal roofs. While taking shelter from a passing squall we ate a shore lunch in one of the deserted huts. Inside we discovered a vagabond's diary that had survived many years. It described the brutal weather conditions of the area, especially during winter.

Entrance areas to some of the shacks were adorned with bones of whale and/or walrus, and some had a tall holding pole for the collection of caribou antlers. (Photo by Terry Manthey)

(Photo by Terry Manthey)

Challenged by the area's forceful winds and tempestuous weather patterns, terrestrial wildlife managed to flourish. Overlooking the forsaken village an extended family of fidgety fox braced against the harsh winds in search of food and the welcome sound of an approaching bush plane. By association, the sound of a plane's engine meant easy scavenging of fish parts left by anglers. From atop its den location the fox surveyed daily a forgotten landscape.

A brisk wind whistled an ancient tune through a nearby wood-planked fishing boat embedded in sand at shoreline. Tilted to one side near the edge of the river it screeched of a proud ancient culture lost to the perils of war. Variations in sound were produced by wind passing through the boat's open-cavity hull. The wood-ribbed shell performed as a reed instrument of history, in honor of a more vibrant time.

Another pungent reminder of a healthier period was our discovery of an unearthed wood-planked casket containing skeletal remains of a Native villager. The historic placement of a cemetery adjacent to a high bank above the river did not warrant against eventual erosion of the peninsula's sandy soil. Over time an encroaching river diminished the burial ground boundaries. The same river that provided sustenance for the living had shown impertinence toward the dead. Approximately six feet below the upper riverbank edge was a fully revealed, mostly opened wood casket. Stripped of all dignity, the intact skeleton inside awaited further exposure as the eroding precipice led only to the flowing river below.

Native artifacts and human remains documented a historic time of brave people who waged battles against the treacherous Bering Sea for whales, walrus, seals, sea otters, and salmon. Brown bear, caribou, and fox highlighted their sustenance-gathering effort for nutritional strength and warmth from the land. More recently, human endeavor on the distant tundra has been limited to commercial setnet operators and sportsmen willing to endure harsh weather conditions and expense necessary to explore a narrow volcanic divide between two unforgiving seas.

A dilapidated trapper's shack was a remnant reminder of a previously healthy Native settlement nearby. Decayed by age, it remained watchful over riverbanks where boyhood ambitions were resurrected.

At the end of our final day of fishing we carefully selected a few silvery brutes with thick, firm flesh worthy of a barbecue and festive commemoration back home. Following the filleting of fish at shoreline an acceptable payment of salmon remains was offered the forlorn fox. Favoring the salmon's head, the fox proudly scampered toward an underground cache with its long awaited prize. Our reward was the fulfillment of two angler's dreams of a distant land with ancient streams and primeval landscapes, and the thrill of catching wild silver salmon to twenty pounds with a fly rod. However, our most cherished memory is of exhilarated, sharing hearts.

ADVENTURE ALASKA

Sourdough Legacy

Prospecting Harbinger Herring

Sport-fishing for tackle-busting salmon among Alaska's remote river systems did not prepare me for commercial netting of bait fish in open water. It was my good fortune to experience the intense fishery with dedicated men and women prospecting slippery silver nuggets along open shoreline waters of the Bering Sea. An invitation to join the harvesting of roe herring from a good friend, activist, and president of the Bristol Bay Driftnetters' Association, Dan Barr, was tantalizing to the bite. Hooked by the attraction of a unique adventure opportunity, I agreed to serve as a crewman for my friend on his thirty two foot salmon gillnetter *Slam Dunk,* meaning a "sure two-pointer" in basketball jargon. Occasionally, a sockeye salmon would flip over the power roller and fly nonstop straight into a brailer liner bag. "Ka-fump" — a slam dunk. An "easy score" was "in the hole," or holding bin, for later transfer to a processor (tender).

Swift-traveling schools of herring numbering countless millions can bring relief to many. The silver horde's heralding role is well established. For the commercial and sport-fishing communities, these early-season harbingers announce the prized salmon's pending arrival. Salmon migrations are influenced by a healthy presence of returned herring. The diminutive bait fish are a rich food source to ravenous salmon cruising open sea shorelines prior to homing in on its river of origin. Once salmon enter fresh water, the burden of sacrifice is initiated by replacing feasting with fasting.

Other predatory marine wildlife with equally voracious appetites depend on the return of herring. Whether perched on high cliffs, wallowing in crowded shorelines or lurking in the darkness of the deep, anxious eyes and sensitive nostrils search the distance. Glittering surface disturbances indicating massive mushrooming movements of bony bait fish beneath signals the end of a predacious wait. The herrings' arrival is met with clamorous activity from above. Clear skies darken with a myriad of screeching marine birds. Beaches holding walrus and sea lions empty. From below, predator attack is relentless as the blue water undulates with flashing silver.

Waves of metallic bright herring are not the prey of gluttonous marine marauders alone. However, eating pleasure of the small fish is not why brave sea gamblers are lured to an open sea to roll the dice, or gillnet drum (reel). As a target fishery, the quest in prospecting a herring resource is about logistics and a lucky turn of the drum. The sought-after motherlode is appropriately carried by the female herring as roe, and must fulfill the ripeness requirement of the Japanese consumer market. Because of narrow parameters for success, risk capital entrepreneur fishermen know the commercial uncertainty of each day's promise and each season's success.

My spring arrival at the fishing village of Naknek in Southwest Alaska was accompanied by a large number of investor fishermen anxious to open their seasonal offices on blocks. The Naknek River landscape included acres of dry-dock boatyards filled with aluminum boats sprouting antennas and radar equipment reminiscent of a navy shipyard awaiting a proclamation of war. Most of the predator boats included a large drum of monofilament net for gillnetting operations. A few of the commercial entrees were larger, with a tall pulley mast supporting a draped net for purse seining.

The limited commercial season opening was not imminent, as

waning snow flurries extended winter's confinement. Owners with crewmen were steadfast in assessing the requirements for a successful voyage. Con-

Rows of fully equipped boats appeared foreboding to whatever the object prey might be.

cern for greater efficiency was a preoccupation during days of restless waiting. A son of a carpenter, I assumed the task of raising the floor level on my friend's boat, using large wood planks. Modifications were needed to the stern (rear) section for the gathering of herring. The newly constructed height provided for an efficient scooping of herring into carrying bins below.

While I constructed a more effective area to collect netted herring at sea the captain deliberately worked to revive the motor from winter hibernation.

Exhausted by extensive preparations, and frustrated by opening delays, we moved anxiously throughout several adjoining boatyards discussing strategy with friends of the captain. From the boatyards we traveled short distances using a section of the only dedicated highway on the Alaska Peninsula.

My friend's boat, Slam Dunk, *was a veteran salmon gillnetter.*

The extent of the highway was a distance of fifteen and a half miles, and connected the village outposts of Naknek and King Salmon.

Following weeks of survey flights resulting in repeated postponements, the Alaska Fish and Game announced the sighting of roe herring balls measured not in millions but in miles nearing Togiak Bay. The delayed arrival of hordes of tiny shiny spawners encouraged even the most disheartened. Quick-spreading news created chaotic activity reminiscent of pre-prospecting conditions following early Alaska's announced discovery of gold. In this case, however, the glitter was of silver and to be mined beneath the water surface.

Social gatherings included buffet dinners at Trident Seafoods cannery and an occasional survey of night life in the small village of Naknek.

During the first high tide following the breaking news full boatyards emptied quickly as if the entire holding area had been tilted on edge. Calm water conditions during the night's dark hours provided an armada of sourdough gillnetters and seiners a marine route to riches. The mouth of the Naknek River assumed a congestion reminiscent of the historic Chilkoot Trail during Klondike gold-rush days of the Gay Nineties (1897-1898). A modern day view is that of a freeway commute at workday's end. The fishing fleet of casino hopefuls entered Kvichak Bay and set compass readings for the far reaches of Bristol Bay. A second destination around Cape Newenham to Security Cove of Lower Kuskokwim Bay was also planned. All was within the greater Bering Sea catchment resource region.

The nautical expedition took most of the night. My friend's gillnetter was not built for speed. It required constant charting awareness and electronic navigational alertness while passing through shallow Kvichak Bay, past Nushagak Bay and the Walrus Islands to Togiak Bay. Many hours at the helm were shared in order to maintain a sharp visual compliance with maritime mapping and marine conditions.

Morning's early light on a mirror-smooth Togiak Bay revealed its bordering mountain range dressed in winter's remnant white. Reflected shoreline images were dotted by the presence of a floating flotilla. Calm conditions belied a pioneering purpose of the buoyant encampment. Dedicated to hope's appeal, all had rushed to discover a rich marine deposit of glittering wealth. As the large number of boats with crew began to nervously move for positioning, the previously serene setting became suggestive of a prospectors' tent camp bustling with hurried claims.

One seiner had a floatplane moored to its rear section, or stern area.

Partnering the effort to strike it rich were vessels looming large near the outer edge of the galaxy of smaller fishing boats. The floating processor's role was to tend the needs of the fleet, including collection, assessment, and refrigeration of each successful catch. They were to herring fishermen what assayers, telegraph, and mercantile stores were to original prospectors, or sourdoughs.

Additional delays at sea challenged the most patient in waiting for optimal conditions. All were eager to volunteer in the collection of sample roe herring for testing. The *Slam Dunk* was among several boats selected to lower a gillnet into cold Alaska waters for that purpose. Assessment of the randomly caught herring was done by Fish and Game personnel. The time-sensitive spawning condition of roe herring needed to approach ideal. Only the female herring provided the possibility of success. Male herring were incidental to the highly valued roe carrying females. Every ton of herring later collected in nets and transferred to a waiting processor was evaluated according to the percentage of female roe herring present and its egg maturity.

Among the processors, or tenders, was the Prince William Sound.

Japanese investors dictated the conditions necessary for a profitable return on the fisherman's dedication of money, time, and sweat. The succulent morsels of pleasure were destined for an epicurean palate. Consumers' savory preference in Japan determined the desired ripeness of roe. Because preference in taste is a fickle feature to consider the bar for success was set at a very high level. Considering market volatility, prospecting this unpredictable marine resource during extreme conditions required a dedicated perseverance.

We spent hours at the marine radio receiver waiting to hear a starting gun. When the fleet was finally green-lighted rising fuel exhaust near the water surface signaled revved engines. Racing propellers churned sea water leading to an extensive vein of silver, or holding area for spawning herring. Successful mining of the resource was a matter of locating a potentially productive set location within the holding area. The working environment was highly competitive between gillnetter boats. Activity bordered on frenzy in all directions. Hopeful of staking a claim to a rich supply of roe herring, each crew prepared for a deluge of small slithery spawners onto the stern area while keeping watchful eyes on rival boats.

The unreeling of a long gillnet required diligence. A strategic set of the lengthy aquatic curtain and a bountiful retrieve to transporting bins in a lower section of the boat were not activities for the fainthearted. Picking the mesh of slippery, silvery spoils captured from the sea was a time-critical exercise. Scooping the flooded stern area rich in caviar was a backbreaking task. It was no more arduous, however, than a later transfer of the herring from filled storage bins to a floating processor. Boatloads of herring from each day's set, or sets, were expeditiously conveyed to the tender through a large-diameter siphon hose. The flexible but awkward conduit resembled a giant elephant's trunk, and was capable of reaching the bottom of the deepest holding bin. It was not a simple operation, and required the strength and agility of a NFL (National Football League)

For the successful, a heavily laden boat was dangerously close to dipping below the water's surface, whether starboard or portside.

linebacker. The waiting time for storage transfers was sometimes hours, depending on the fishing fleet's success. Bone tired, wet, and smelling like the fish below, we waited our turn in line. Knowing the difficult chore that awaited the transfer of our catch to the processor we could only imagine the refreshing relief of the tender's warm shower afterward.

A line of moored boats waiting for a dispatching of herring extended the grueling experience.

Strategy, persistence, and good fortune netted a profitable portion of the motherlode for the *Slam Dunk*. Our success provided a rewarding return on my friend's investment. For others, a less productive set location and/or equipment failure offered only dreams of an upcoming salmon season.

Days of buoyant pursuits on a watery frontier gave new meaning to *cabin fever*. Confined, labor-intense conditions during several days at sea encouraged a desire for the firmness and stability of land beyond shore. While ashore we explored solid trails that led to elevated viewing of a rugged, remote coastline. Sheer rock cliffs were the nesting habitat for a variety of marine birds. Cradled high on top of a large protruding rock was the uncommon site of a bald eagle's nest. The rough landscape appeared barren without the lush carpet of summer. It was easy to imagine the brutality of a tempestuous, unforgiving Bering Sea.

Using a small raft we launched a day's diversion at Security Cove. Setting foot on the beach was a reaffirming, grounding experience. (Photo by Dan Barr)

The mountainous rock formations were the only fortress that could withstand nature's cruelty and provide sanctuary along the shores of this distant and solitude tundra region of Alaska.

Captain Dan Barr stands next to a predator's nest positioned to overlooked an immense area including both land and sea. To the west was an extended ocean eventually leading to Russian waters.

Our return passage across an expansive Bristol Bay section of the Bering Sea provided relaxed and enjoyable viewing in surround sound. Orchestrated by nature's baton, a symphony of sounds came from a myriad of screeching cliff-dwelling seabirds seemingly in perpetual flight. Along the rocky shore a community of Steller's sea lions barked a welcoming chorus during our passing. A determined adult was not distracted while instructing a schooling group of frol-

icking young sea lions swimming near our boat. Later, a huge gray whale's spouting *whoosh* directed our attention to a seascape beyond the bow (front) of the boat. The gallant creature's spewed exhale seemed a celebration of relief in completing its lengthy migration north. The grand display appeared symbolic of our own extended journey, and the sat-

A massive male sea lion basked in the warm sun on a partially exposed rock near shore. He demonstrated what appeared to be a position of reign.

isfaction in its success. Beyond the whale's vaporous fountain was our final course to a distant boatyard in Naknek.

ADVENTURE ALASKA

Island Extreme

—— Emerald Gem in Alaska's Gulf ——

A small commuter plane's low-altitude flight across Alaska's treasured emerald island vibrated with a rough, caressing sound. Limited to sight-only instrumentation, the single-prop plane danced with forceful wind currents and swift-moving cloud formations common in the Gulf of Alaska. The hum of its single engine inspired visions of thrilling discoveries in a lost-world setting. Clearings between drifting low clouds exposed sensational vistas of jagged peaks draped with carpets of lush green vegetation. The sights below were of divine influence, and confirmed Kodiak Island's cherished status. The rugged terrain was a natural wildlife sanctuary and established National Wildlife Refuge, where predators reigned. The sloping tundra pointed to cliffs abruptly dropping to icy blue inlets and sparkling fjord-like bays. The visual drama was a relief from distracting high-rise congestion in a developed world, and soothing to the soul. Finally, from the air an open view of our village destination promised a successful landing and visit to paradise found.

The Native village of Larsen Bay, situated in western Kodiak Island on Uyak Bay, was our destination. Uyak Bay is also a popular destination for sport fishermen seeking a "world's strongest man" competition with some of the heaviest barn door halibut in Alaska. Close by are the renowned Ayakulik and Karluk Rivers. Less notable to the sport-fishing enthusiast are the Brown and Zachar Rivers. I was invited to this sportsman's fantasy island to serve as river fishing guide for a resident lodge named after its island location, Kodiak (Lodge). Each of the nearby rivers provided world-class sport-fishing for prolific runs of wild salmon and exposure to the drama of a remnant primeval setting.

Opening to Shelikof Strait, the area's salmon fishing industry supported a historic cannery facility during the summer.

The cannery commissary supplied island needs for seasonal employees, many of which were from Russia.

Nearby was a nautical graveyard for previous generations of pioneering commercial vessels used in supplying the cannery.

During my tenure as guide, the marine alternative of Uyak Bay provided up close sightings of surfacing whales, playful porpoises, and sea otters. The lodge manager, Bob Maschmedt Jr., was also a skilled boat operator and fishing guide for halibut and salmon entering the bay. A typical day's catch included robust salmon and halibut of unusual size, both instinctually groomed for nature's call to spawn. For the fortunate lodge guest, the stout salmon and hefty halibut were destined to serve an epicurean delight. The savory smell of smoked salmon and pleasurable taste of white-flaked halibut from deep, cold northern waters was the reward at day's end. For family and friends back home the dream continued.

Wildlife viewing pleasures distinguished each guided trek into the bowels of a remote island jewel. Among a potpourri of incidental adventure snapshots were skittish Sitka deer, curious fox, and watchful bald eagles. The main attractions were countless scurrying salmon heading upstream to fulfill a promise and the world's largest land predator intent on terminating the spawner's mission. Both were determined to satisfy one of nature's requirements for survival, although different from the other. The odds for individual success was weighted heavily in favor of a gorging Kodiak brown bear. Sacrifice was inevitable for the salmon, even though countless numbers of surging messengers of new life guaranteed a successful return upstream in spite of marauding bears.

During river fishing expeditions I was astonished by regular sightings of Kodiak Island's famed brown bear, considering its preference for solitude. Kodiak Island is regarded as a safe haven for these colossal carnivores, named after the place they inhabit. There is approximately one brown bear for every two square miles of island habitation. The Kodiak brown bear is a mammoth subspecies, or *super species,* of other brown bear in the grizzly family. It is the jumbo-weight sumo wrestler of grizzlies, and is without equal in all parts of Alaska and elsewhere. Its gargantuan size evolved from countless generations of high-protein consumption from rivers and streams filled and lined with an unending source of salmon. A large male can reach ten feet in height standing on its hind legs, and a weight of 1,500 pounds. Other creature activities on the island proceed with an intimidating awareness of the bear's omnipresence.

As a fishing group we acknowledged the need for a respectful regard when inviting ourselves to a brown bear's shoreline spread. Prudence in distinguishing between intimidator and exterminator was essential to our advance upstream. To witness a looming behemoth standing upright to smell for scent other than salmon was to be impressed with the stature of such a gigantic beast. It was always an awesome spectacle, especially when the bear was standing only a few yards from our position in the river. Although a long established island fortress of the bear, our intrusive maneuvering upstream seemed marginally acceptable.

A shallow, musty smelling Brown River supplied the nutritional needs for a concentration of celebrity carnivores, large even for Kodiak Island. The river's namesake identified these congested meat eaters competing along its banks. The sight of layered fish carcasses covered with silt below water level, and the smell of rotting remains littering the length of its shorelines challenged the imagination. To visiting anglers, the primeval view with its pungent odor of decay distinguished the ancient river as unaltered by the ages.

Left behind by the boat operator at high tide, I cautiously led a group of fishermen into the primitive time capsule setting. Images were of a lost-world environment. Considering the territorial instinct of bears, our only advisable approach to fishing the river was the river itself. Fresh signs along the river's edge were preliminary to eventual sightings, and encouraged the highest degree of vigilance and calm. While wading midstream, the pervasive odor of countless dead salmon decomposing along the shoreline seemed incongruent with such pristine surroundings.

The distraction of foul air was quickly dismissed when we discovered yearling cubs playfully foraging migrating salmon. Innocent of savage aggressiveness, the curious siblings pounced in shallow water to the beat of new discoveries. It was a pleasantry not often observed in such extreme conditions for survival. The playful display was under the watchful protection of an imposing mother capable of a ferocious defense of her cubs. Consequently, the exuberant cubs seemed distracted only by the relentless swarming of mosquitoes.

In contrast, we soon observed a less carefree young adult male pioneering a nearby territory without the security of a guarding mother. Predictably, the protective instinct of the small cubs' mother and the young male's uncertainty of territorial privilege led to confrontation. An intolerant mother quickly approached the tentative young male nearly its size. Primitive posturing and spine-chilling sounds seemed precursory to a fierce exchange leading to mortal combat. Both bears' gaping mouths undulated, exposing flesh-tearing teeth capable of delivering severe consequences. The ground resonated from beastly guttural roars, suggesting a savage prehistoric display. I was astounded by the intensity of the conflict, while was not cruel or destructive. The bears' instinct exhibited an aggressive style intended to avoid rather than inflict serious injury. Although both bears appeared intensely threatening, the mother delivered a saliva-secreting proclamation easily understood by the yielding young male. The stage for violence dramatized instead a wild display of domination by intimidation.

Another fishing expedition to the upper Brown River required the same midstream route. We were again accompanied by hundreds of streaking pink salmon avoiding our predator image above. Matted bear grass trails followed the edge of the narrow river on both sides, and did not invite even the frivolous. Heavily used territorial pawpaths were for bears alone. Leftover gnawed salmon lay in compressed grassy locations along low banks. The toll for human access to these paths of privilege would likely be too high a price to pay. A mauling of the curious on uncertain trails where the height of bear grass easily concealed a sleeping giant was a daunting consideration.

Two anglers from the fishing group were interested in exploring farther upstream to a known holding area for migrating silver salmon. While trudging against the current we observed looming above the river surface ahead two impressive creatures. The tall, dark images were standing upright, attempting to identify our scent downwind by smell. Silhouetted against the glistening river and silver-gray sky, the bears' forelegs and paws dangled while noses bobbed to reach some confirmation. A nearly adult cub mimicked its mother's every move. Their height appeared an awesome sight, giving the illusion of a river shrunken in size. Unable to determine our scent because of the wind direction both bears dropped to all fours and defensively scurried up a high bank, uncertain of possible predator intent.

Impressed with the imposing display we proceeded with extreme caution. Once past the position vacated by the mother and cub a more favorable wind direction assured the bears that we did not pose a formidable threat. Relieved by the changed conditions, the bears returned to the river. As a dominant inhabitant of the island the mother reasserted territorial rights, knowing our position upstream and on the food chain. Without further incident the bears' gorging for winter needs continued.

Following a successful fishing experience for salmon and Dolly Varden, decidedly catch and release, we ate a shore lunch before beginning our midstream return. As we approached the feasting bears position in the river the mother was watchfully linked to our every move. An invitation to the all-you-can-eat salmon buffet included only her less experienced offspring. As the uninvited we approached nervously, yielding to the bears dominance. To avoid riling the bears' fury we appeared consoling by using a passive wading technique and spoke in a normal tone. The wisdom in our catch and release activity upstream earlier was now evident. A backpack cache of salmon might have tempted bears with ravenous appetites supported by territorial privilege.

The narrow width of the river required us to pass close to the mother's protective instinct, and without gifts to bear. Our exit route was well known as harm's way. Courage and patience were essential during our gradual advance past the bears position in the river. The potential volatility of the mother did not diminish the need for our persistence. Refuge at the mouth of the river was a great distance. Timing our return was critical, leaving no alternative but to continue. At low tide river access would become a cascading waterfall to the bay. A boat awaited our return at high tide.

At our nearest passage to the feasting bears we hugged the riverbank as the mother appeared less forbearing and more distressed by our intrusion. Her irritability seemed elevated, with little attention given to eating. With a menacing posture the mother moved toward our tense edging along the opposite bank. The cub followed its mother as the grizzly pair advanced toward our untenable position. No longer able to retreat, I lowered a protective gun from my shoulder while maintaining an acceptable distance between us. Readied for a distressful moment in time, I continued to counsel the mother to accept our marginal imprudence while slowly advancing downstream.

The mother appeared dangerously contemplative of our advance downstream. An impulsive charge, commanded by instinct, seemed a moment away.

Relief came after being escorted some distance from the bears' banquet on rocks. With some trepidation we acknowledged a profound gratitude for having felt the pulse of the pristine and the untamed that inhabit it. Our courageous earlier advancement upstream and later return provided a wild experience without provocation, and worthy of recall. When rejoining the remainder of the fishing group downstream we learned that a large adult male brown bear had crossed the river near their location. The male's presence and direction upstream explained the protective mother's nervousness and instinctual security check earlier.

Whereas a brown bear's instinct embraces strong protective and nurturing qualities, a lesser known characteristic is its developed intelligence. Moments to marvel at a masterful display of learning occurred at another island river location. Only during high tide could we reach the upper end of an inlet leading to the remote Zachar River. An early morning excursion across a smooth-surfaced Uyak Bay offered a reflective time of anticipation.

Glassy water conditions enhanced an indelible image of Kodiak Island's primitive charm.

The serene seascape and pristine landscape appealed to the soul. Along the rugged inlet shoreline scavenging fox and Sitka deer were easy to spot from the boat. The visual ensemble included frolicking sea otters swirling and splashing nearby. Others were backfloating while feeding on mollusks caressed against a furry stomach. A widespread distribution of discarded shells from the nutritional mining of oysters and clams contributed an element of intrigue to the inlet's shallow end during low tide. Layered deposits of shell sediment with an endless aquatic shelf life laid on the bottom as evidence of an undisturbed past. Stepping from the boat onto the shallow inlet's calcium carpeted bottom, we forged through crystal-clear water to a secluded beach.

As we loaded backpacks on each other we felt the exhilaration of discovery leading to wild silver salmon stacked in river pools. Fishing gear in hand, we embarked on a wilderness trek in anticipation of a momentous adventure. Our passage from the inlet shoreline opened to a wide, grassy area with estuaries regulated by nature's dramatic fluctuating tides. After traversing mudflats and streambeds during lower tide conditions we cautiously hiked through tall grassy vistas with increased excitement. Primitive paths aged by the trampling of bears did not acknowledge time's advance. Steaming scat (bear feces) on the trail confirmed our visitor status, and the need for courage in facing the uncertain. Great bald eagles perched on towering snags were watchful of our careful advance. Every precaution to not wrangle the bears' conditional hospitality was observed. A prudent concern for safety, however, did not diminish our pleasure in viewing the wonders of a primitive world setting. We were further rewarded when reaching a cool, welcoming upriver shoreline.

The wild habitat of the Zachar River was less intimidating than that of the Brown River, although similarly remote. We extended extreme caution to the riverbank regardless of its less threatening appearance. While we were preparing rod, reel, and selected tackle, the brawny keeper of that section of river strolled along a rocky shoreline in a consenting manner. We were obliged to the bear for its hospitable gesturing. Autumn's backdrop to the surveillance movement of the bear included resting colors of yellow and gold reflected on glassy water surfaces of large pools. The picturesque canopy ensemble concealed hundreds of migrating silver salmon awaiting a later surge upstream. The river's virgin setting was scintillating to the senses as each fisherman's dream carried thousands of miles was realized.

One of the author's trophy silvers kept for shipment home. (Photo by Bob McCan)

After successfully fly-fishing several transparent pools stacked with resting silvers, the small group of cautious fishermen moved downstream. Remaining behind, I continued to fly-cast into holding pools with an angler from Winston-Salem, North Carolina. Although ambivalent, the spin of remote Alaska's roulette wheel rewarded Bob McCan's decision to remain upstream. We soon understood the proprietor bear's beguiling greeting earlier. Near the extended measure of our back-casts we heard a crunching sound. Turning quickly we witnessed up close a winner's surprise. The startling jackpot view was of the wily resident brown bear with the weight of silver draped from its mouth on both sides while clamped in the middle by large, purposeful canines.

The cunning humped male had silently edged onto a log overhanging a clear water holding area behind our fly-casting position. Reaching down with long razor claws the brown brute grasped one of the large silvers tied to a limb. Fastening its vise-grip jaws around the girth of one of the salmon the crafty bear pulled the fish from a stringer rope with one unyielding head jerk. With the draping salmon firmly positioned in smiling jaws, the raunchy host celebrated a satisfying return on his investment in forbearance.

There was no mistaking the bear's intelligence in assessing our contribution upon arrival.

Although willing to share some of the salmon as booty, I was certain of the bear's continued appetite to plunder. Following a first serving, the gorging giant would return for a second silver-plate special. A swift salvage of the remaining silvers confused the pensive bear's later search for the fish. With the slow movement of Goliath the robust creature wasted no additional energy while knowing the reward for patience. Sitting a short distance beyond the length of our back-casts the shimmering blond bully anticipated that a lavish nutritional gratuity of salmon carcasses (minus separated rich fillets) and fish eggs would be left behind.

The visiting sportsman of fortune was startled by the impressively stout bear's up close appearance. Alarmed, the gentleman guest felt uncertain of the pillaging carnivore's intention beyond savoring the salmon appetizer. Facing a scrounging bear for the first time, he felt no buttress from the river behind him. Remaining mild-mannered, he nervously inched downstream along the shoreline while questioning our user-friendly status and distinguishing *cautious* from *careless*. Later downstream we turned to witness our grizzly landlord dining on the spoils of persistence.

The occasion was not the bear's gain alone! For us, the bear's clever display extended beyond the wilderness event. Grateful hearts will forever pound an exhilarated beat from the discovery of a secluded wilderness extended from time's beginning. Our fortuitous encounter with such a majestic wild creature was destiny's reward for surrendering to the unpredictable in adventure's call.

A separate and final expedition required a low-elevation float-plane ride over remote habitat from Larsen Bay village past the Karluk River to the Ayakulik River. Except for a seasonal tent camp sighted along the upper river the view was of a solitary landscape. Our destination was a pristine but forbidding section of Kodiak Island, known for its prolific salmon runs. The bush plane's sound alarm for touching down announced a water landing near a bank along the Ayakulik River.

Following the unloading of fishing gear on shore, the pilot expressed his concern about a strong weather front rapidly advancing into the region. Because the turboprop Beaver de Havilland was flown by sight instrumentation only, a success-ful later pickup was uncertain. With collective bravery we waved a hopeful return to the pilot as he taxied the river for lift-off.

It was a courageously dedicated pilot who maneuvered the plane to a successful river landing, especially upon his return.

The day was mostly exciting for each fisherman, landing acrobatic silvers with fly rod and tackle. While welcoming home a few of the finning faithful, each angler kept a watchful eye. The shorelines of the Ayakulik River are renown for hefty brown bear inhabitants. Eventually, fighting salmon on the end of fly lines were easily noticed by strolling resident bears.

Well equipped to brawl, but presumably nutritionally satis-fied, the brawny host with cubs remained only curious of our ecstasy. (Photo by Terry Manthey)

Cold, rainy conditions and the uncertainty of the floatplane's return by nightfall diminished our enthusiasm near day's end. While waiting for the plane's return, the wet chill replaced a stimulating warmth from each calculated cast and aggressive strike. Later, we became more contemplative as the weather worsened, encouraging us to huddle together on the riverbank. There was no escape from the deluge along the distant tundra shoreline.

Following an anxious time of discomfort and uncertainty, relief was recognized in the far away hum of a plane's engine. Spirits lifted as the serenading sound strengthened, confirming our rescue. In the distance two dim lights pierced dense, shrouded conditions. Seemingly stalled in a motionless sky, a misty winged form moved through a thick, vaporous blanket. Soon, the ghostly appearance of a welcomed floatplane came into view. Tracking the river below, the pilot searched along the riverbank for a few drenched souls. Spotlights mounted on each wing pierced a dismal haze suspended above the narrow river surface. Emerging from the obscurity of a semitransparent curtain of gray, the plane's return dispelled all thoughts of cold, wet, and sharing the shoreline at night with a grizzly host.

Loaded with fish, gear, and shivering fishermen, the weighty floatplane needed to gain enough air speed for lift during a near-windless condition. Repeated taxiing on the calm river surface resulted in a precarious lift-off. When airborne, our visually impaired return to the lodge included other close-call flight maneuvers while traversing several mountains, causing tense moments and later appreciative hearts.

The protruding emerald island gem set in Alaska's gulf offered each dedicated fisherman and spirited adventurer a fascination with the primitive. For myself, it was also a unique opportunity for close encounters with wild Alaska's dominant player, the Kodiak brown bear.

The ferocious disposition and voracious appetite demonstrated by bears throughout the island's wilderness reach was also observed in its less dignified role as omnivore. The village garbage dump at Larsen Bay was a trash delight providing "meals on wheels." For nature's raunchy opportunists, plundering daily banquets in boxes offered the attraction of a lavishly prepared buffet. Young and old were exposed to the resolve of every other salivating freeloader, although an enforced hierarchy stabilized a crude assembly. During summer's evening twilight the dump arena became a cautiously competitive setting reminiscent of Olympic class super heavyweights during warmup.

The variety of creature personalities and role distinctions exhibited within the welfare community of carnivore underachievers seemed a familiar human condition. As an observer of exchanges between Kodiak Island's dominant predators surviving ancient times, I was able to learn more of the savage and nurturing in man.

ADVENTURE ALASKA

Highway to Heaven

—— From Hope to Heaven's Gate ——

Much of nature's drama staged throughout bush Alaska was also available in areas having road access, albeit with a much greater human audience. Each highway expedition was compelling to the adventurous and artistic spirit, replicating the awesome splendor of remote Alaska's rugged spectacle.

Turnagain Arm's noble setting is a crown jewel preserved for the admiring romantic.

The visually stimulating Turnagain Arm subinlet of Cook Inlet provides the only highway access to outdoor opportunities of privilege south of Anchorage. The subinlet is an environmental jewel cradled between the Chugach Mountains to the north and the Kenai Mountains to the south. It is a picturesque water corridor accompanied by subalpine glacial valleys with meadows of lavender and passion-pink fireweed pointing upward to stunning icy-blue glaciers and cascading waterfalls in search of sparkling tide flats below.

The surrounding glacier-endowed grandeur confirms the magnificence of the wild, and man's folly in abusing it. Both sides of the shimmering corridor proudly showcase mountains regimented by nature to defend the subinlet's treasured resource. Elevated peaks often pierce an advancing shadowy veil that shields nature's resolve below.

During an overcast day bright sprays of sunlight sifting through swift-moving clouds highlight the inlet's glistening silver-gray surface of water and mudflat designs below.

Glacial monuments gracing the mountainous passageway are also spectators of Turnagain Arm's bore tide spectacle. Because the area boasts a tide differential of as much as thirty-seven feet, low tide conditions expose miles of picturesque mudflats. Occasionally, the unusual phenomenon can fill the subinlet in a single wave, requiring extreme caution. The resulting tidal flood is formed by rapidly incoming water colliding with outgoing water, and can roar to six feet in height and move at speeds to fifteen miles per hour. I was eyewitness to the infamous tidal advancement while attempting one final cast for silver salmon near the mouth of Bird Creek. Nearby fishermen were unable to avoid its stealthy approach and needed assistance to survive the frigid deluge.

Included in the kaleidoscopic wilderness setting is the historic mining town of Hope. It was easy to imagine Alaska's early sourdough digs while visiting the turn-of-the-century gold rush community. The visual background drama was a timeless display that extended its golden history. Since its fame and brief fortune, Hope's transformation has been from panning gold to casting for deposits of silver and pink. Resurrection Creek runs through the townsite and is a homing attraction for large numbers of silver and pink salmon. Miner's cabins have given way to vacationer's needs. From the tucked away settlement's only boardwalk café the fruity aroma of freshly baked blueberry pie was savored by the nose and later confirmed by its warm, succulent sweetness.

During a clear autumn day along Turnagain Arm the changing colors in leaves of aspen, birch, and willow showcased the other rich deposit left behind in Hope and elsewhere. Golden leaves shimmering against a sky of royal blue complemented protruding mountains streaked and spotted with rich colors from nature's palette and veiled by autumn's first snow. The spectacular seasonal display proclaimed summer's end.

A parade of wildlife performers from the curious to the unyielding stretched the length of the Kenai Peninsula. Discovered among the less submissive was a resolute female brown bear working the pristine, turquoise-colored upper Kenai River shoreline. The super-sized grizzly was fishing mostly by collision, as it was positioned in the instinctual aquatic path of sockeye salmon migrating upstream near shore. Not yet knowing of patience, nearby energized cubs swayed with bobbing heads while playfully bouncing up and down against large rocks with forepaws. They appeared intermittently curious of mother's determined technique in submerging for food. A plentiful supply of salmon added contentment following sporadic displays of youthful aerobic exercise. The mother's blonde fur shimmering against a morning sun modeled the magnificence of wild Alaska's nurturing giants.

Following the breakfast buffet of fresh sockeye, satisfied cubs carried full stomachs to the top of a tall tree overhanging the river. It was a rare occasion when the large mother followed a short distance in monitoring her two cubs. Only a smaller black bear is known for climbing skills, regardless of age. Soaring high above the grappling siblings, a great bald eagle with keen eyesight did not require the same closeness to its indifferent river prey. Predator instinct from such a height selected only the careless fish swimming near the river's surface. Without hesitation, strong talons of the swooping symbol of freedom fastened tightly to its morning meal. With water cascading from the captive fish at lift-off, it was to learn in the end of new heights in nature's drama.

A zone of feverish activity upriver challenged the ecstasy of a wilderness ecosystem. In what is popularly referred to as combat zone fishing, eager fishermen were slotted together to form a line reminiscent of civil war advancement. Dedicated anglers were relentless in flogging the current while maintaining a restricted position near shore. It seemed uncertain which species was in greater danger, the unsuspecting sockeye salmon moving upstream or the tenacious combatants homesteading the shoreline. Scores of fishing rods were pointed toward midriver with rod tips bouncing from weighted lines against river bottom rocks. Drifting lines with salmon flies attached searched the current's depth hopeful of an inhaled take by a gaping-mouthed, nonfeeding red salmon. Intermittent proclamations of "Fish on!" encouraged the less fortunate in an adrenaline rush promoting perseverance.

For a section of the fishing regiment, weariness from casting and retrieving was subdued by the appearance of a formidable brown bear on the far riverbank. The large sow stood upright with scouring nostrils pointing at a few remaining nearby anglers willing to risk uncertain danger. Fortunately, it was the nutritionally satisfied mother with cubs seen earlier. Harm's way, however, was only slightly diminished by the protective mother's full stomach. Intrepid fishermen wading the far shoreline knew only of the bear's presence, and not of its contentment or maternal intent. The two inquisitive cubs remained curious of the partially submerged anglers attempting to pillage their feeding grounds. Earlier, a similar view of their mother positioned near shore was an invitation to food. On this occasion, satisfied stomachs limited their response to cub curiosity. Secure in the closeness of mother's protective watch, the cubs continued along the river shoreline in search of new discoveries. For the wary fisherman, vacillation between nervous excitement and a consideration of retreat preempted fishing expectations.

Later, a short distance from the same opposite shoreline a cow moose and young calf were seen forging the swift current. A comrade fisherman indicated that a week earlier the same moose lost a second calf during a hazardous crossing. With her one remaining offspring, the mother was instinctively determined to cross at the same location, regardless of the previously lost calf, similar water conditions, and the human barricade ahead. Although moose swimming toward a blockade of fishing fanatics seemed less alarming than the meandering brown bear with cubs, protective mothers of both species can become violently aggressive when irritated.

Savage attacks by bulky brown bears using large canine teeth with crunching, vise-like effect and saber-like claws that spread the width of its large forepaws for slashing are well documented. Less renowned are menacing assaults by a usually tranquil, awkward-appearing adult moose when provoked. While tenaciously defending its young, a previously indifferent moose becomes a cruel assailant. Its use of spearing forelegs with pounding hooves is relentless. Even the fierceness of a hungry brown bear is tempered by the prospect of injury during a tempestuous defense by an adult moose. Viewing these wilderness monarchs required an alert eye and a respectful distance. For ambitious sport fishermen wadding in line along the upper Kenai River, courage, caution, and courtesy were important considerations.

Favoring a more solitary experience, I left the marauding multitude and their flailing of fishing rods behind. A reconnaissance by road resulted in my return to an area previously discovered. From a high elevation the view was of a secluded basin surrounded by glacial mountains. Undisturbed waterways below again beckoned a pursuit of the wild in wilderness. A trailhead sign warned of recent brown and black bear activity along the trail to the valley floor. Memories of past visits to the remote fishery at trail's end, however, outweighed warnings of a possible bear encounter. A cautious stride was established hiking down a sloping, narrow path. With eyes searching in all directions, self-consoling conversation in a normal-tone and rattling bear bells attached to my hiking boots proclaimed my visitor intent. Fortunately, only steaming scat on the trail threatened my quest for solitude.

Undeterred by the bear's recent deposit, I soon became absorbed in the vigilant fulfillment of a promise. Throughout the small valley's marshy entrance wild iris in purple regalia patrolled the stream's migrating parade of fatigued salmon returning from the sea. A bulky bull moose appeared unimpressed as it lifted its weighted head from feeding below the stream's placid surface. Water that was lifted by a widely-spread, spooned rack cascaded past an elongated muzzle to its source below. Glaciers beckoned the eye from a distance, while high above in a sapphire sky a bald eagle's flight extended the serene condition below.

For this occasion, a camera was selected over a fishing rod.

Where the stream flashed red, pairs of spawning salmon danced with an instinctive urgency of purpose. At the same wilderness nursery the raunchy returnees had years previously hatched as fry. As smolt, they later began a delayed, dangerous journey downriver to Cook Inlet and the Gulf of Alaska. Following years of nutritional gain in the open sea, as mature adults they surrendered to instinct's final call to return to the place of their beginning. The journey was mapped by sensory imprint. An acute sense of smell was the directional force in retracing the salmon's previous route downriver.

For the returning salmon, a shallow current cupped in a wilderness basin was willed by heaven.

The successful return home was commemorated with a final watery waltz. Streaking dorsal fins in shallow water created V-shaped wakes. Swirling action provided spawning bed impressions in gravel known as *redds*. It seemed the ultimate persuasion of instinct's call to surrender. Procreative rights were available only for the most vigorous. A crowded assembly of wounded warriors left behind a multitude of less fortunate sibling hopefuls. Contemplative, I surmised the odds of battered survivors successfully maneuvering through countless perilous attacks. Killer whales, sea lions, seals, northern pike, bears, ospreys, eagles, commercial trollers and netters, and sport fishermen were among the predator hazards. The homecoming was a testimonial to luck, endurance, and a commitment to the fulfillment of a promising future through sacrifice.

The once prodigious male salmon became a fierce-appearing pursuer. Pronounced morphological changes had stripped the fish of its streamlined silver luster. The skin showed a sacrificial red coloring. A grotesque hook for an upper jaw prevented the mouth of the spawning male from closing. Sharp canine-appearing teeth were visible in the upper and lower jaws. The snout, ragged tail, and fins were splotched in white where decomposition had already begun. Its energy reserve was depleted and fungus colonized its softening body.

Digging a gravel bed nest (redd) by spawning salmon was followed by the female's release of eggs. A shivering discharge by a male completed the fulfillment of a future. Near the gravel bedding area was the ominous company of scurrying hopefuls. Rainbow trout and Dolly Varden char were the final entry on the salmon's predator list. The aquatic jackals patiently waited to pillage the watery nest of succulent, fertilized eggs. Defense of the spawning bed area was necessary to drive the smaller opportunists away from the deposited eggs. Occasionally, an intimidating charge by a nearly spent parent toward an egg snatcher left the protein-rich spoils to the more cunning in waiting.

Eventually, the protective instinct of the salmon was diminished to futile breathing attempts through clogged gills, leaving the nests vulnerable. Like tenacious vultures awaiting certain death, darting trout and char persisted until the demise of the salmon was certain. Flaccid and with eyes that searched no longer, the salmon's instinctive commitment to renewal through sacrifice extended nature's drama to another season. Lying motionless near its deposited legacy of fertilized eggs, the carcass was a fleeting memorial to perseverance. The sunken remains would later provide the nutritional need for a new generation of salmon. What was once a place of beginning had become a place of final triumph, and beginning again.

Following a time of winter incubation, newly hatched fry would again transform the stillness of decay into a gravel nursery playground. The requirement of surrender would be replicated with every advancing offspring instinctually driven to sea and back. At the upper trailhead marker I imagined my excitement would come from catching and releasing salmon. At trail's end I was grateful of the greater reward awaiting me on that occasion.

At the highway's farthest reach south a picturesque bay harbors a rich marine resource. Rugged mountains divided by glaciers and steep-sided fjords complement the prized ecosystem of Kachemak Bay. Angler success suggested a seemingly unlimited number of halibut cruising the bay's bottom. I was amused by an aquacade of frolicking sea otters near the boat. Several fidgeting, long whiskered mollusk and crustacean eaters swirled on the water surface as if performing. Others floated on their backs, some in order to support and feed their young. The serendipitous displays served a respite from baiting hooks and cranking reels, while humorous one-liners from a cursory comedian, captain Larry Connolly, continued throughout.

During my adventurous pursuit of treasured discoveries was a stunning disclosure. Passion's pleasure rose to a height of soaring eagles. It was extended beyond arched fishing rods and the depth of the bay's bottom feeding halibut. Experiencing the spectacular was no longer limited to impressive wildlife scenery and sport-fishing drama.

Introduced was a sweet exchange that satisfied desire's thirst with ecstasy. The rising tide of affection would later reveal during emotion's ebb tide a cleansing of debris from sandy shorelines past. Two playful souls with similar lusts for adventure were stimu-

Thrilling fishing excursions for halibut enhanced a peninsula adventure that approached Heaven's delight. (Photo by Thu Autumn Ly Idle)

lated by a seductive sea during the day and a sensuous full moon shinning softly between veiled layers of wispy low clouds at night. Subtle dockside sounds during nighttime's restless-calm serenaded tentative but seeking hearts. For both, an unlatched door leading from fear's solitary confinement opened wide for passage to freedom's call to closeness. Electric moments charged by warm hands and wistful eyes sparked a new beginning. Mature hearts softened by the tenderizing of time encouraged a ripened connection. A passionate dawn extended pleasure's cause. Indelible memories spiked by radiant colors of autumn would preserve summer's savory serving for two. Concern of spoiling was limited to the halibut harvest from beyond land's end.

While returning to Anchorage along the corridor expanse of Turnagain Arm, a viewing area provided a consuming calm. White porpoise beluga whales often forage schools of hooligan (candlefish) at this location. Named after the ghost-like mammals, Beluga Point also provides viewing of bald eagles feeding on silver-ribbed mudflats at low tide, and Dall sheep on steep, craggy mountainsides next to the highway.

Summer's late night sun seemed suspended in its setting position. Images seemed clearer and colors more vivid. The subinlet's glassy water surface, shimmering mudflats, and bordering mountains reflected a divine dance of rich colors choreographed from above. Shades of orange, peach, pink, and purple combined to stimulate the visual while transcending the personal. Profoundly heartfelt, such imposing splendor humbled my human spirit.

Twilight's glow extended a stimulating, colorful display originating at Heaven's gate. The peninsula adventure had been a spectacle bonanza, an alignment with nature's wondrous world. Feeling nourished by discovery's gain, all expectations sought in life seemed a fulfillment away. Inspiration was more than sensuous. During an evening of blissful revelation I understood passion's call to be the pursuit of pleasure's greatest reward, a soulful journey. The heart desires no other destination! As an adventurer, photographer, artist, and lover, I hold dear this unifying celestial prize.

A new beginning,
A reason for living,
A deeper meaning,
I want to stand with you on a mountain,
I want to bathe with you in the sea,
I want to lay like this forever,
Until the sky falls down on me ...
            Savage Garden, 'truly madly deeply'

ADVENTURE ALASKA

Dogged Determination

Heart and Soul of Alaska

*When I need some time alone it's a place where I can go,
'Cause I share my dreams with the caribou and the
whisper of the wind.*

*Seen the giant grizzly and the salmon as they run,
And all of nature's wonders in the seven months of sun, ...
And heard the barking of the huskies calling me.*
                              - Lee Greenwood, 'Home to Alaska'

Epitomizing the adventurous spirit that discovered and settled America's last frontier is the renowned 1,150 mile marathon running of the Iditarod Trail Sled Dog Race. *The Last Great Race* is named after the historic outpost of Iditarod, meaning *A Far Distant Place*. The remote ghost town is located next to a river by the same name, and along the famous trail that memorializes its prosperous and charitable past. The Iditarod trail originally served as a mail and supply route and a wilderness conduit for enterprising gold mining sourdoughs.

The present-day annual marathon race between Anchorage

at Northern Cook Inlet and Nome at the coastline of the Bering Sea replicates the trail's historic route between those locations. The incomparable Iditarod event honors a limitless frontier with a caring past, and exemplifies Alaska's heart and soul. More than a race, it is a commemoration.

In 1925 dog teams and mushers with fearless bravery and stamina used an extended winter trail (mid-January) across the breadth of Alaska's wilderness. Beginning in Seward on the shoreline of the Gulf of Alaska eighteen heroic sled dog teams relayed serum needed to save the Yup'ik Eskimo village of Nome from a diphtheria epidemic. In 1973 the celebrated Iditarod Trail challenge was initiated in memory of the great historic humanitarian effort. Incredible courage demonstrated by mushers and sled dog teams during the famed Iditarod race for survival remains a standard for today's frozen trail rivalry.

Pitted against the jaws of wild Alaska's winter, dedicated participants must discipline themselves and their sled dog teams for racing uncertainties during severe weather conditions, including subzero temperatures. Survival gear for both musher and sled dogs are carefully packed prior to the start. Treacherous trail conditions through forbidding terrain of dense forests, obstacle mountains, frozen rivers, desolate tundra, and miles of windswept coastline along Norton Sound tests even the most dedicated and daring. Hazardous climbs and twisting descents, loss of visibility and direction from blizzards or blowing snow, and melting water surfaces that do not support the weight of a sled team are some of the challenges. Reported encounters with petulant moose on a frozen tree-lined trail and the sighting of polar bear along the arctic coast near Nome are illustrative of a race that is only possible in untamed Alaska.

Dogged determination is an Iditarod race requisite where finishing is extremely difficult. For some, the distance is less than to the finish line in Nome. Days of monotonous solitary miles leads to restlessness, boredom, fatigue, sleep deprivation, and dehydration. Sickness and delirium may require the aid of a racing competitor along the trail. For a few, the measure of a raucous race is adjusted to become a life-saving rescue. For the frigid far north gladiator who is unable to persevere against the trail's extreme and hazardous conditions, ambition and confidence must wait another year.

Hopeful mushers must exercise carefully learned sled-handling and dog-care skills essential for reaching Nome. Tension among impatient sled dogs prior to the start and harness-pulling efforts that challenge physical limits during the vigorous contest influence racing performance. Although considered the strongest draft animal per pound, inbred ambition can be compromised by fatigue during severe deep-freeze conditions. Occasionally, while numb from lack of sleep a musher will loose contact with a dog's mental state, resulting in team mutiny. A lay-down strike by individual dogs can quickly spread to the whole team, resulting in a disappointing no-finish.

It has been suggested that the hardest-working dog on the team is the musher, although most mushers would disagree. Much of the race is run during nighttime's plummeting temperatures when exhausted mushers know only darkness, bitter cold, and the dedication of a few harnessed faithful. A moonless night's landscape is narrowed to vistas of rising vapor from panting canine competitors illuminated by a musher's single headlamp. A brighter moonlit trail reveals ranges of shimmering snow beyond the silence of passing shadows. With either, icy deposits crystallized on lashes of tired eyes and men's gnarly facial hair are indelible memories of the hearty.

Volunteer pilots fly a sky-trail to shuttle supplies and move veterinarians and race officials between checkpoints along the sled dog trail.

The uncompromising care of sled dogs is essential to the sensitive spirit of an Iditarod trail race. Each dog is carefully monitored for endurance at every checkpoint and mandatory rest stop along a trail that extends to the finish line in Nome. At the discretion of attentive mushers and examining trail veterinarians some canine competitors are removed from a dedicated dog team that seeks only the reward of acknowledgment. Small bush planes on skis are used to return exhausted and/or ailing sled dogs to major pickup locations.

The spirit of adventure harnessed to a passion for excellence is the Iditarod. Affectionate teamwork between musher and sled dogs during extremely challenging conditions outweighs in value whatever gold remains at the finish line. Guts and stamina translate to tired ecstasy during the traditional approach to the finish line in Nome, known as the *finish chute*. For the fortunate musher, walking alongside a reduced but resilient sled dog team while acknowledging the cheers and adulation of an appreciative crowd is the culmination of a ten-to seventeen-day grueling journey. For the no less courageous musher who with his or her team passes last beneath the famed burl arch stationed above the finish line, the traditional Red Lantern Award is given.

Upon concluding each Iditarod Trail Sled Dog Race the prestigious Leonhard Seppala Humanitarian Award is presented to the musher who best demonstrated exceptional care of his or her team. Voted on by trail veterinarians, it is given to the musher with the healthiest and largest number of remaining dogs arriving in Nome. Among mushers the award is revered as a notable accomplishment, and is celebrated along with top place finishes.

The musher I volunteered to help is an honored recipient of the Iditarod humanitarian award. Lynda Plettner was recognized for her diligent caring effort in crossing the Iditarod Trail 2002 finish line with thirteen happy, line-pounding dogs. Other teams arrived in Nome with as few as six remaining sled dogs.

A consistent Iditarod finisher, Lynda has starred in the movie *Sled Dogs: An Alaskan Epic*, and appeared in a special television presentation on *Secrets of Alaska's National Parks*. She prepares for the Iditarod year round, and is one of Alaska's highly respected sled dog trainers. Plettner Kennels also provides for the care of retired sled dogs and serves as a popular tour destination during summer months. Lynda loves participating in the Iditarod, and finishing with the big dogs.

The Iditarod is very special to me. It brings me to a new level in my life. It is the race that allows people who love the outdoors and wilderness to have the experience of a lifetime. It is a place you know nothing about until you go. It is an opportunity to get into the wilderness of Alaska and see the country like you never imagined. The land is unforgiving, and not accessible without the (Iditarod) race route. It is too many miles, too far between. You learn to deal with what goes wrong, on your own. Out in this vast, great land you have countless hours of daydreaming. You hear the steady whisper of the runners, the clicking of the dog's snaps, the pitter-patter of their feet, and the sound of their steady breaths. The Iditarod is Alaska, up-close and personal. It has become my vacation with the dogs I raised and trained, my best friends, traveling 1,150 miles in perfect form and loving it.

Lynda Plettner

My enriching experience began while volunteering at the Plettner Kennel mushing boot camp in advance of the celebrated winter race. The boarding and training location is near other kennels run by popular Iditarod mushers, including Martin Buser and Dee Dee Jonrowe. I felt privileged to participate in both routine kennel operations and the starting events of the running of the Iditarod winter spectacle. The kennel grounds housed communities of sled dogs that were separated by stands of birch and a hierarchy based on age and performance. Grooming chores were often accompanied by a frigid far north sunrise that radiated a colorful welcome across snow-blanketed terrain. Inspiration and its warming effect transcended the challenge of icy cold conditions.

Rivaling canine choirs howled a harmonious mood between lot locations. The barking was infectious between encampments, like spontaneous cheering that undulates around a crowded sports stadium. Sharp outcries announced every wilderness entry to the day's frozen stage, from a bald eagle's surveillance flight to a distant return of an exercise sled team. The renditions soon became distinguishable. Often it was a transition from arousal to resignation. Usually, a support cast of cheerleading dogs observing the selection and departure of an exercise sled team were unified in barking a vociferous message. However, the clamorous barking was diminished to a howling, seemingly forlorn group following the team's leaving.

Fisher, Retired Iditarod Lead Runner

Steamy breath from barking sled dogs carried upward a morning message of excitement and anticipation. All were incited by companion hoopla and a heart-throbbing instinct to race.

Ojibwa, Iditarod Lead Runner

Amid a wonderland of white each groomed, genetically driven sled dog awaited a harness and the trail's racing surface beneath its paws.

In addition to caring for a feverish community of selectively bred competitors through feeding and sanitary supervision, kennel-keeping duties included the introduction of timid young dogs to a staging area of experienced racing sled dogs, including members of the Iditarod team in training. The fate of these submissive, unsuspecting pups would be compromise, devotion, and competition. Depending on genetic genius, the skill of a trainer, and the dedication of a musher their destiny could also include fame. Tentative but playful, each young critter appeared instinctively focused on racing paraphernalia and the demeanor of veteran canine competitors. While nervous and uncertain, each future trail warrior extended large untested paws toward the handler for reassurance. A comforting, affectionate response seemed encouraging to the youthful canine thoroughbreds in an insecure world of high expectations.

Each potential lead dog learns a proper response to commands including *haw* for turning left, *gee* for turning right, *on by* for passing or going straight, and *whoa* for slowing down and/or stopping. Beyond verbal directives shouted from the

135

distance of a trailing sled, line-connected anchors punctuate and enforce a holding position along the trail once stopped. For the young in waiting, intelligence, eagerness to learn, and development of strength determine eventual positioning along a racing gangline.

Handler chores prior to practice runs included placing a harness on each dog and securing it to a tugline spaced along a gangline that was connected to the sled. Colorful booties were fitted onto the paws of each dog for protection. The spirited symbiosis created between musher and dog team during exercise runs was essential at race time. It was a critical alliance that encouraged mutual dependency and aspirations. Bonding

The ceremonial start was similar to a spirited pep-rally that attracted locals and tourists to the grand spectacle along Anchorage streets. The official start was one day later in Willow.

along the gangline by multiple pairs of sled dogs was also necessary for a successful racing experience. An eager team of eight pairs, or sixteen dogs, was skillfully trained daily by Lynda in anticipation of the Iditarod Trail Sled Dog Race.

An affectionate working relationship between mushers and the dogs that serve them is manifest in specially selected names given to each. For Lynda's deserving Iditarod 2004 team it was *Apache, BMW, Brumby, Denali* (leader), *Kiwi* (leader), *Lennon, McKinley* (leader), *Noppers* (leader), *Nutella, Ojibwa* (leader), *Outi, Patches, Sacagawea, Scout* (leader), *Snow White, and Termite.*

It was an exciting opportunity for me to serve as musher handler during the ceremonial and official starts of Iditarod XXXII. The ceremonial start was a festive occasion where competitors, including musher icons, and their teams were displayed and honored in an atmosphere of sporting camaraderie.

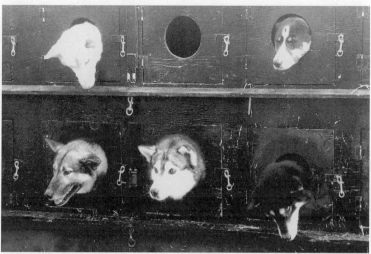

The sled dog team was patient in waiting its time to receive accolades from musher, handlers, and an appreciative crowd.

Prior to the Iditarod official start each compliant animal was transformed into an intensely aggressive teammate. Once a racing harness was placed on each dog and attached to the tugline no further coaching was necessary. Characterized by incessant barking and surging movement forward it was clear that engines had been started and were revved. Competitive juices stimulate sled dogs to feats of tremendous strength and endurance. Restraining a team of sixteen spirited sprint warriors while approaching the start position required a joint Herculean effort by several handlers.

I was curious why the pulling sled dog team included both males and females. It seemed logical that a full complement of

(Photos by Toshiko Ihle)

Prior to the official start, one of the lead sled dogs, Denali, receives a caressing moment of encouragement.

larger, stronger males would provide greater endurance and speed. According to Lynda, both males and females are necessary along the racing gangline because sled dogs are highly developed social creatures. Opposite-sex socialization encourages greater motivation, camaraderie, and energy up and down the line. The smaller, less muscular female competitor tends to persevere during harsh conditions when fatigue often constrains the larger, less focused male. The combination of male and female sled dogs, including some from the same family, generates a more hearty performance. It is

(above) Proud, and with inspiration gained from a year of dedicated preparation, planning, and exercise, Lynda's beloved family team sprint from the official starting line. (Photo by Toshiko Ihle)

(right) Miles of trails did not diminish the bravery of heart and soul in pursuing Iditarod's challenge. (Photo by Jlona Richey)

commonly believed within the mushing community that the mixed-team arrangement encourages a more durable, dependable, and dashing experience.

A companion event to the annual Iditarod Trail Sled Dog Race is the Fur Rendezvous. Both the Iditarod ceremonial start in Anchorage, and the official restart one day later in the Matanuska-Susitna (MatSu) Valley are climactic events of the festive Fur Rondy. While exemplifying Alaska's miners and trappers heritage, the winter carnival resembles the fanfare and frivolity of a frozen far north Mardi Gras. Both celebrated happenings stirs the spirit to seek its own reward by honoring the history of a wild frontier landscape.

> *If you love the grandeur of nature – its canyons, its mountains, and its mightiness, and love to feel the thrill of their presence – then take the (Iditarod) trip by all means; you will not be disappointed. But if you wish to travel on 'flowery beds of ease' and wish to snooze and dream that you are a special product of higher civilization too finely adjusted for this more strenuous life, then don't. But may God pity you, for you will lose one thing worth living for if you have the opportunity to make this trip and fail to do so.*
>
> *C.K. Snow,*
> *At the End of the Trail,*
> *(BLM-Alaska 'Adventures in the Past' Series, No. 6)*

Lynda Plettner's website:
http://www.plettner-kennels.com

ADVENTURE ALASKA

Unity in Diversity

Winter's Allure
and
Summer's Prolific Embrace

Alaska's harsh winter conditions have long been the subject of written narratives, artists renderings, and cinema portrayals. For this author and environmental romantic, winter's extreme is showcased by a seemingly endless mantle of brilliant to shaded white. Craggy mountains emphasize the diversity of shadowing while cradling numerous glaciers that extend winter's frozen confinement. Lower landscapes include legions of standing aspen, birch, and willow naked against a cold blue sky and distant sun. Stripped of summer's dignity, shadow lines from the sleeping upright trees are cast across smooth drifts of scintillating snow, confirming the impression of a low orbiting sun along the southern horizon. Radiant sprays of light also permeate top sections of interspersed evergreen spruce adorned with jeweled crowns of sparkling white. Silhouetted against a penetrating sun the stately conifers stand in regal splendor, adding to daytime's glistening spectacle of brightness.

Alaska's cold elegance is often enhanced by a delicate tint of pink spread across its terrestrial face. Blended into a snow-packed canvas landscape, the most vivid alpenglow coloration is viewed on mountains facing afternoon sunsets. The profuse pink (representing quality and excellence) phenomenon is created by a far north sun's low trajectory. Nature's good taste in colorful displays of a magical sun is extended to nighttime's mysterious illuminating influence. A prolonged winter night's lunar-celestial ensemble is occasionally upstaged by awesome swirling ribbons of dancing northern lights (*aurora borealis*). The sometimes lengthy curtain call display appears in an infinite sky laced with varying shades of chartreuse or red above a sleeping snow-laden horizon.

Winter's charming views of the terrestrial and heavenly complement a variety of serendipitous discoveries. A statuesque moose ponders slow-motion strides in a thick blanket of angelic white from above. The same soft snow is an erratic speedway for the scampering camouflaged hare. Stagnant sounds of silence and swishing quickness identify the contemplative moose and frivolous hare. In contrast, teams of resolute sled dogs demonstrate a more resounding effort in seeking the finish line at trail's end. Children explore a generous playground of fluffy white. The sight of steam rising from thermos cups is further evidence of memorable family pleasures found in the crisp stillness of a frozen landscape. Like an alluring full moon, winter's drama is warming of the senses.

Springtime in Alaska releases winter's icy grip. *Breakup* during spring is a dramatic clashing of natural forces. From snow covered frozen surfaces to fragmentation and floating ice, resulting moonscape appearing inlets and rivers suggest a mother's duress at delivery. The transformation to summer's ecstasy is a time of celebrated renewal. The raven's stark winter caw is replaced by harmonious honking of returning geese in low-level formation. Above the gliding geese a hurried hum from bush planes, both float and wheeled, can be heard in response to summer's awakening call.

The season's invitation to embrace a warm recovery does not include any reference to a frozen past. Everywhere exploration flourishes with a recreational pursuit of new discovery. There is no denying the migrating salmon a purpose-ful effort, or the devoted fisherman his or her quest. Summer's rejuvenating short season is a beckoning call to the dedicated adventurer. Men and women revisit riverbanks of childhood expectations. With rod in hand they seek to restore passion's extended past. For children, it is an awakening to passion's extended future. For both, it is uncertain if even the northern summer solstice can provide sufficient time for the fulfillment of a youthful heart's desire.

The need for precaution against winter's piercing edge melts with warming opportunities for outdoor pursuits. Movement is extended, as are daylight hours.

A near midnight sun provides prolonged days of growth, yielding berry shrubs that erupt in sweet surrender. Succulent tastes and seductive fragrances highlight summer's invitation to the savory senses. Wildflowers adorn a resurgent landscape of incredible design. Caressed by an extended sun, the flowery habitat exhibits a tapestry stitched with color, including hues of yellow, blue, pink, purple, and lavender. Prolific displays of arctic lupine and Alaska's state flower, the alpine forget-me-not, are generously painted on summer's canvas from nature's palette of mixed colors. Lavender-pink fireweed dominates the wild landscape display as if strongly squeezed from nature's reserve. Standing in regiment, the erect, flowering plant appears to patrol with passion.

Lone Fireweed in Foreground

Alpine slopes, woodland meadows, marshes, and bogs exhibit summer's appetite for color.

Both the frozen spectacle of Alaska's sparkling winter white and summer's radiant warmth of flowing colors are enriching to the soul. Each is an inspiring manifestation of natural beauty. The spectacular occurrences of winter and summer are a tandem display. Winter's cold splendor is alluring, and the unveiling of summer's bliss offers a warm embrace. As one follows the other, allure and embrace characterize the unity in Alaska's diversity.

Epilogue
—— A Last Frontier ——

Developmental congestion and pressures of financial security are often intrusive to an individual's spiritual space. Community sprawl encourages complex living conditions that can cause estrangement, including from nature. Indifference often breeds confusion about our internal and external worlds. Concerns of affection, purpose, and fulfillment are sometimes replaced with feelings of detachment, arrogance, or issues of survival. For the sensitive individual with a delicate capacity for feeling, growing uncertainties can erode confidence. Personal and economic security issues resulting from expanding high-density growth worldwide, and cultural ideological differences threaten all that is inalienable. Warmongering invades the sanctity of life, and reduces expressions of freedom to restrictive provisions of license.

A postgraduate trainer of mine, psychiatrist Alexander Lowen, wrote regarding "The Truth of the Body" in his book *Love And Orgasm* that progress engenders an environment where productivity replaces inspiration, and spontaneity gives way to compulsion. Lowen suggests that neither knowledge, wealth, nor power has meaning unless it contributes to the well-being and enhancement of the individual. Through dissatisfaction man realizes that the joy of living may be escaping him. When life's mysteries are reduced to a formula or subdued by commercial interest, man is stripped of passion.

For the disheartened, to surrender to passion's call is as likely as walking on the moon. A pilgrimage to the unknown or unpredictable is often discouraged by comfort's needs. Painful contractions resulting from discomfort favors ease over enrichment, or expansion. For these less adventurous, the manicure appeal of a gated community carved into dry, bleached desert sand in the Lower 48 is a less daring alternative to Alaska's extremes. Wearisome sameness and artificial design are the rewards offered a sedentary person who knows only the distance to the moon, and not its magic.

The path leading to a more vibrant life is discovered at the trailhead marked *PASSION -Proceed with Fullness of Heart.* To possess a passion for the last frontier is to imagine the wonder in wild. To experience passion *as* a last frontier is to seek the sensuous in its pursuit. It is to learn of tenderness in the untamed and feel stimulated by its discovery. Strong feelings are a rich inheritance given to the sentimentalist seeking life's loving embrace.

Pursuing Alaska's valued resource was once an effort to line the prospector's purse with gold; now, it is to feel the pulse of renewal through discovery. Where wild remains a guarded treasure, life's adventurous quest reaches beyond the security of enlightened dogma, polished promises, or glistening stones. Modern day frontiersmen explore regions that transcend geographic and social boundaries. These are the vanguards of a soulful journey. Curious and courageous, they know pleasure's fullness in pursuing the sensational. For the adventurer seeking footprints to follow, one small step or one giant leap requires less travel than to the moon.

Heartfelt experiences are coveted by all who seek a serendipitous path to travel. I am grateful for untamed horizons that have stirred to action a curious quest. Spontaneous reaching out and taking in has led to greater aliveness. To feel deeply is to know a compassionate, purposeful connection to the world, and is nourishing to the soul. Yielding to passion's call to surrender expands the boundaries of both courage and pleasure, and is the invitation and destination of the heart.

Sharing my adventures on passion's table is intended to massage the spirit. Embracing Alaska's frontier environment arouses within profound emotions and soulful insights. Magnificent natural resources and cultural charms are an awakening to pleasure's purposeful pursuit. Documenting my discoveries of fortune extends the gift of vicarious pleasure to all seeking through discovery a more adventurous life.

The pleasure in being fully alive is realized in the movement of the unpredictable and unprecedented, leading to love's fullness. It encourages an ambitious transformation from irritation to inspiration. It is a freedom song sung by all who shun fear's restraint and cherish adventure's challenge. Pleasure's freedom song is sung by the bold and brave, and was written about throughout this narrative by a sensitive romantic.

ON PLEASURE
Pleasure is a freedom-song,
But it is not freedom.
It is the blossoming of your desires,
But it is not their fruit.

It is a depth calling unto a height,
But it is not the deep nor the high.
It is the caged taking wing,
But it is not space encompassed.
Ay, in every truth, pleasure is a freedom-song ...

... it is the pleasure of the bee to gather honey of the flower,
But it is also the pleasure of the flower to yield its honey to the bee.
For to the bee a flower is a fountain of life,
And to the flower a bee is a messenger of love,
And to both, bee and flower, the giving and the receiving
of pleasure is a need and an ecstasy.

ON LOVE
Love gives naught but itself and takes naught but from itself.
Love possesses not nor would it be possessed;
For love is sufficient unto love.

When you love you should not say, 'God is in my heart,'
but rather, 'I am in the heart of God.'
And think not you can direct the course of love, for love,
if it finds you worthy, directs your course.

Love has no other desire but to fulfill itself.
But if you love and must (needs) have desires, let these be
your desires:
To melt and be like a running brook that sings its melody
to the night.
To know the pain of too much tenderness.
To be wounded by your own understanding of love;
And to bleed willingly and joyfully.
To wake at dawn with a winged heart and give thanks for
another day of loving;
To rest at the noon hour and meditate love's ecstasy;
To return home at eventide with gratitude;
And then to sleep with a prayer for the beloved in your
heart and a song of praise upon your lips.
                    Kahlil Gibran, THE PROPHET

Appendix

—— Author's Oil Paintings ——

Alaskan Artist Finds Renewal

Alaska has provided me an opportunity to experience the preserved grandeur and intrigue of a last frontier. During the short days of winter I have spent time in my studio bringing to life cherished moments using paintbrush, palette knive, oil medium of color, and canvas. My oil paintings replicate spirited views of a preserved culture and its land, and are painstaking in detail and realism. Each painting represents an extended period spent in my studio.

Friendship and trust established between myself and special Yup'ik and Aleut friends, John and Mary Tallekpalek, allowed me to roam freely their subsistence fish camp during visits. I captured their historic lifestyle on film, and later on canvas. The Tallekpaleks practiced the old ways of the Levelock people. The land has remained pristine while the culture has incorporated change through compromise.

Good things come in time! The oil paintings presented on the following pages and the completion of this adventure narrative exemplifies the value of patience and perseverance.

Wild Sunrise, Branch River, Southwest Alaska

Moose Forging the Branch River

Mary Tallekpalek Filleting King Salmon with Ulu Knife

Salmon Drying Rack, Branch River Fish Camp

Salmon Carcasses, Branch River Fish Camp

Native Siblings, Goodnews Bay/River

Branch River Sunset

Kenai Peninsula Pursuit

A Setting on Earlier Times

Author may be contacted regarding oil paintings,
additional copies of *Pursuing the Untamed*,
book signings, and public appearances at:
AdventureAlaska_Ltd@yahoo.com.